First World War
and Army of Occupation
War Diary
France, Belgium and Germany

33 DIVISION
Divisional Troops
Divisional Ammunition Column
11 December 1915 - 14 June 1919

WO95/2413/8

The Naval & Military Press Ltd
www.nmarchive.com
Published in association with The National Archives

Published by

The Naval & Military Press Ltd

Unit 10 Ridgewood Industrial Park,

Uckfield, East Sussex,

TN22 5QE England

Tel: +44 (0) 1825 749494

www.naval-military-press.com

www.nmarchive.com

This diary has been reprinted in facsimile from the original. Any imperfections are inevitably reproduced and the quality may fall short of modern type and cartographic standards.

© Crown Copyright

Images reproduced by permission of The National Archives, London, England, 2015.

Contents

Document type	Place/Title	Date From	Date To
Heading	WO95/2413/8		
Heading	33rd Division Divl Artillery 33rd Divl Ammn Colmn. Dec 1915-Jun 1919		
Heading	33rd D.A.G. Vol 1 Dec 15 Jan 19		
War Diary	Bulford	11/12/1915	11/12/1915
War Diary	Southampton	12/12/1915	12/12/1915
War Diary	Havre	13/12/1915	14/12/1915
War Diary	Aire	15/12/1915	15/12/1915
War Diary	Berguette	23/12/1915	23/12/1915
War Diary	Ligny-Les-Aire	24/12/1915	24/12/1915
War Diary	Berguette	16/12/1915	22/12/1915
War Diary	Ligny	25/12/1915	31/12/1915
Heading	33rd D.A.G. Vol. 2		
War Diary	Lingy-Les-Aire	01/01/1916	03/01/1916
War Diary	Linghem	04/01/1916	28/02/1916
War Diary	Vendin-Lez-Bethune	29/02/1916	30/04/1916
Heading	Officer i/c Ag Office At The Base		
War Diary	Vendin-Lez-Bethune	01/05/1916	30/05/1916
War Diary	Bethune	31/05/1916	30/06/1916
Heading	War Diary Divisional Ammunition Column, 33rd Division July 1916		
War Diary	Bethune	01/07/1916	07/07/1916
War Diary	Cantrainne, Etc	08/07/1916	10/07/1916
War Diary	Le Mesge Soues Crony Hangest	11/07/1916	12/07/1916
War Diary	Lemesge	13/07/1916	13/07/1916
War Diary	Near Treux	14/07/1916	14/07/1916
War Diary	Becordel	15/07/1916	31/07/1916
Heading	33rd Divisional Artillery 33rd Divisional Ammunition Column R.F.A. August 1916		
War Diary	Becordel	01/08/1916	06/09/1916
War Diary	Bonnay	07/09/1916	07/09/1916
War Diary	Naours	08/09/1916	08/09/1916
War Diary	Bois Bergue	09/09/1916	09/09/1916
War Diary	Milly	10/09/1916	10/09/1916
War Diary	Lattre St Quentin	11/09/1916	16/09/1916
War Diary	Guadiampre	17/09/1916	17/09/1916
War Diary	Coullemont	18/09/1916	23/09/1916
War Diary	Lattre St Quentin	27/09/1916	06/10/1916
War Diary	Coullemont	08/10/1916	19/10/1916
War Diary	Couin	20/10/1916	22/11/1916
War Diary	Talmas	23/11/1916	23/11/1916
War Diary	Bellifontaine	25/11/1916	26/11/1916
War Diary	Allery	27/11/1916	30/11/1916
War Diary	Carnoy	08/11/1916	08/11/1916
War Diary	Daours	09/11/1916	09/11/1916
War Diary	Argoeuves	10/11/1916	10/11/1916
War Diary	In The Field	01/12/1916	31/12/1916
War Diary	Bray-Sur-Somme	02/01/1917	02/01/1917
War Diary	Vaux-S-Somme	03/01/1917	03/01/1917
War Diary	Longpre Halt	04/01/1917	04/01/1917

War Diary	Conde	07/01/1917	22/01/1917
War Diary	Camp XIV	22/01/1917	22/01/1917
War Diary	Vaux-(East Of Suzanne)	23/01/1917	29/01/1917
War Diary	L.16.B Bray	01/01/1917	01/01/1917
War Diary	Camp 14	02/01/1917	02/01/1917
War Diary	Vaux	03/01/1917	03/01/1917
War Diary	Longpre Halt	04/01/1917	04/01/1917
War Diary	Longpre-S Saint	15/01/1917	15/01/1917
War Diary	Argoeuves	16/01/1917	16/01/1917
War Diary	Vaux	17/01/1917	17/01/1917
War Diary	Camp 112	19/01/1917	19/01/1917
War Diary	L.10.B.	23/01/1917	23/01/1917
War Diary	Vaux	07/02/1917	07/02/1917
War Diary	Bray-Sur-Somme	14/01/1917	28/01/1917
War Diary	Bray La Motte-Brebiere	11/03/1917	11/03/1917
War Diary	La Motte-Brebiere	25/03/1917	25/03/1917
War Diary	Naours	27/03/1917	27/03/1917
War Diary	Beauvoir-Riviere	28/03/1917	28/03/1917
War Diary	Honval	29/03/1917	29/03/1917
War Diary	Habarcq	30/03/1917	03/04/1917
War Diary	Duisans	04/04/1917	06/04/1917
War Diary	Arras	09/04/1917	31/05/1917
War Diary	In The Field	01/06/1917	30/06/1917
War Diary	Boiry-St-Rictrude	03/07/1917	23/07/1917
War Diary	Orville	24/07/1917	24/07/1917
War Diary	Dunkerque	25/07/1917	25/07/1917
War Diary	Ferme-Du-Nord	26/07/1917	31/07/1917
War Diary	Coxyde-Bains	05/08/1917	12/08/1917
War Diary	La Panne	15/08/1917	02/09/1917
War Diary	Les Moeres	03/09/1917	03/09/1917
War Diary	Wemaers-Cappell	04/09/1917	04/09/1917
War Diary	Reninghelst	11/09/1917	25/09/1917
War Diary	Dickebusch (Near)	26/09/1917	30/09/1917
War Diary	In The Field	01/10/1917	31/10/1917
War Diary	Hubertshoek Near Dickebusch	03/11/1917	05/11/1917
War Diary	Bavinchove Near Cassel	06/11/1917	08/11/1917
War Diary	Bavinchove	11/11/1917	12/11/1917
War Diary	Haut Loquin	15/11/1917	02/12/1917
War Diary	Wemaer Cappell	03/12/1917	03/12/1917
War Diary	Vlamertinghe	08/12/1917	27/12/1917
War Diary	Poperinghe	29/12/1917	30/12/1917
War Diary	Busseboom Near Poperinghe	01/01/1918	08/01/1918
War Diary	Vlamertinghe	09/01/1918	22/01/1918
War Diary	On March To 4th Army Rest Area	30/01/1918	31/01/1918
War Diary	Merck St Lievin	01/02/1918	20/02/1918
War Diary	Renescure	21/02/1918	21/02/1918
War Diary	Vlamertinghe	22/02/1918	31/03/1918
Heading	33rd Divisional Artillery. 33rd Divisional Ammunition Column R.F.A. April 1918		
War Diary	Vlamertinghe	01/04/1918	10/04/1918
War Diary	Dranoutre	11/04/1918	11/04/1918
War Diary	Kokereele Camp Westoutre	12/04/1918	15/04/1918
War Diary	Canada Corner	16/04/1918	16/04/1918
War Diary	Reninghelst	18/04/1918	18/04/1918
War Diary	Houggraaf	19/04/1918	19/04/1918
War Diary	Reninghelst	20/04/1918	20/04/1918

War Diary	Poperinghe (1 M.W. Of)	25/04/1918	30/04/1918
War Diary	Poperinghe (1 Mile West Of) 27/L.10 Central	04/05/1918	15/05/1918
War Diary	Proven (1 Mile S.W. Of)	18/05/1918	27/05/1918
War Diary	Staple	01/05/1918	01/05/1918
War Diary	Bandringhem	02/05/1918	03/05/1918
War Diary	27/K.15.D.8.2	04/05/1918	04/05/1918
War Diary	27/L.14.C.8.7	09/05/1918	09/05/1918
War Diary	27/L.14.C.8.7	05/05/1918	05/05/1918
War Diary	Proven (1 M.S.W Of)	06/06/1918	06/06/1918
War Diary	Abeele (About 1 M. N.Of) (27/L.13.B.5.0)	14/06/1918	28/06/1918
War Diary	1/ 1/4 Mile N. Of Abeele (27/L.13.B.5.0)	03/07/1918	06/07/1918
War Diary	Poperinghe (1 M. North Of)	20/08/1918	29/08/1918
War Diary	Proven (Near)	31/08/1918	31/08/1918
War Diary	Canettemont (Near Frevent)	01/09/1918	02/09/1918
War Diary	Louvencourt	14/09/1918	14/09/1918
War Diary	Beaulencourt	15/09/1918	16/09/1918
War Diary	St Martins Wood	17/09/1918	17/09/1918
War Diary	Frevent	28/08/1918	29/08/1918
War Diary	Milly	15/09/1918	15/09/1918
War Diary	Acheux	16/09/1918	16/09/1918
War Diary	Bazentin Le Grand	18/09/1918	18/09/1918
War Diary	Le Transloy	20/09/1918	20/09/1918
War Diary	V.14.A.9.9	27/09/1918	27/09/1918
War Diary	27/K.18.B.9.6	20/08/1918	20/08/1918
War Diary	Zeggers-Cappel	21/08/1918	21/08/1918
War Diary	Est-Mont	26/08/1918	28/08/1918
War Diary	Est-Mont	27/08/1918	27/08/1918
War Diary	St. Martins Wood	22/09/1918	22/09/1918
War Diary	Manancourt	28/09/1918	29/09/1918
War Diary	Heudicourt	30/09/1918	24/10/1918
War Diary	Montay	05/11/1918	05/11/1918
War Diary	Englefontaine	06/11/1918	06/11/1918
War Diary	Le Grand Pature	07/11/1918	07/11/1918
War Diary	Sarbaras	11/11/1918	14/11/1918
War Diary	Croix	15/11/1918	15/11/1918
War Diary	Clary	16/11/1918	16/11/1918
War Diary	Lesdain	18/11/1918	06/12/1918
War Diary	Equancourt	07/12/1918	07/12/1918
War Diary	Meaulte	08/12/1918	08/12/1918
War Diary	Pont Noyelles	09/12/1918	09/12/1918
War Diary	La Chaussee	10/12/1918	10/12/1918
War Diary	Andainville	12/12/1918	12/12/1918
War Diary	Neuville	21/12/1918	31/12/1918
War Diary	In The Field	18/01/1919	31/01/1919
War Diary	In The Field	03/01/1919	03/01/1919
War Diary	Neuville-Coppegueule	08/02/1919	11/02/1919
War Diary	Neuville-Coppegueule	07/02/1919	12/02/1919
War Diary	Neuville-Coppegueule (Somme)	01/03/1919	31/03/1919
War Diary	Neuville-Coppe (Somme)	17/03/1919	17/03/1919
War Diary		01/04/1919	30/04/1919
War Diary	Gamaches	16/05/1919	14/06/1919

WO87/2413(8)

33RD DIVISION
DIVL ARTILLERY

33RD DIVL AMMN COLMN.
DEC 1915 - JUN 1919

33RD DIVISION
DIVL ARTILLERY

33rd STR.
Vol: I

/C/
7935

Dec '15
June '14

WAR DIARY 33rd Divl Ammn Column

or

INTELLIGENCE SUMMARY.

(Erase heading not required.)

Army Form C. 2118.

Hour, Date, Place	Summary of Events and Information	Remarks and references to Appendices
11th Decr. 1915 = Bulford	Left BULFORD in 8 trains for SOUTHAMPTON en route for HAVRE. Good journey and very little trouble considering newness of the Unit. Three-quarters of personnel embarked in SS. BELLEROPHON and a quarter on ARCHIMEDES.	W.J.
4.30 p.m. 12th Decr. Southampton	Set sail for HAVRE escorted by two torpedo destroyers.	
13.12.15 = HAVRE 14.12.15	Arrived and disembarked HAVRE. Proceeded to neighbourhood of BETHUNE in 3 trains on 13th and 14th. Headquarters and a portion of No.1 Section turning up the rear.	W.J.
4.15 p.m. 15.12.15 = AIRE	After travelling since 8 am on the 14th, Headquarters detrained at AIRE between 4.15 pm and 6.15 pm. After march of about 6 miles the Column concentrated at the village of BERGUETTE, becoming of 15th. Men had braked extremely well under new (and some to many, trying) circumstances. No casualties except a few minds injured on board ship. This train was a very superior arrangement to S. fry a D.A.C. of 4 Divisions and the insufficiency of not much hampered by insufficiency of room of quarters. The miserable inability of French Railway Stations make entraining (and entirely) slow and difficult. Very necessary to detail special parties and not let men more about the lemos this Column should be detrained from a lorg force now, in Short, of a platoon of a Coy, drawn by men they are likely and	

Army Form C. 2118.

WAR DIARY
or
INTELLIGENCE SUMMARY.
(Erase heading not required.)

Instructions regarding War Diaries and Intelligence Summaries are contained in F. S. Regs., Part II and the Staff Manual respectively. Title pages will be prepared in manuscript.

Hour, Date, Place	Summary of Events and Information	Remarks and references to Appendices
THURSDAY — 23.12.15. BERGUETTE	Capt. Smith & Mr Edwin accompanied the S.C. R.A. 33rd Division to RELY and LIGNY-LES-AIRE to choose new billets for us. In the afternoon took the Section Commanders out to meet the above but failed to find them.	Very wet day. [initials]
FRIDAY - 24.12.15. LIGNY-LES-AIRE	Marched to LIGNY-LES-AIRE and went into billets. The Co. and Subjects went on early to make final choice and mark billets. Head of Column left BERGUETTE at 10 a.m. The new "N" SECTION and attached LIGNY at 1.30 p.m., passing by MAZINGHEM and FONTES to avoid flooded roads. No. 2 Section did not get out of Wagon Lines till midday and even then Ligny and wagons behind Workshops overturned in a ditch. Owing to the delay and further mishaps on the road the last wagon of No. 3 SECTION did not reach LIGNY till after 3 p.m. and our wagon was left in BERGUETTE till the under-carriages broken by the assistance of the men. No 2 Convoy was left in the road-way and the Wagons for the night. All other were parked by 5 p.m. The mile of road between Ligny and BERGUETTE has by far, can never be safe as is fearfully heavy & supply of Army is four deep heels — scarcely than Drinking places for horses our & possibly fruits by farmyard drainage. At this season there is no firm hard ground cover than under the waterlogged fields.	

(7.3589) W141141—463. 400,000. 9/14. H.&J.Ltd. Forms/C. 2118/10.

Army Form C. 2118.

WAR DIARY
or
INTELLIGENCE SUMMARY.
(Erase heading not required.)

Instructions regarding War Diaries and Intelligence Summaries are contained in F.S. Regs., Part II and the Staff Manual respectively. Title pages will be prepared in manuscript.

Hour, Date, Place	Summary of Events and Information	Remarks and references to Appendices
Thursday 16.12.15 - BERGUETTE	so that the drivers may take themselves and horses and hook on. Similar procedure for tomorrow. Got orders from R.A.H.Q. but not their address. All arms and men in billets at 10 p.m.	Weather fine & cold. W.J.
Friday 17.12.15 - BERGUETTE	Spent the day inspecting and allotting billets. The G.O.C. R.A. visited the unit with a view to ascertaining the state of billets, horse lines and parks. A scheme for improvements as to be put forward.	W.J.
Saturday 18.12.15 - do -	Nothing to note	Weather foggy W.J.
Sunday 19.12.15 - do -	Sent 51 wagons to TREIZENNE to draw Howitzer Ammunition for 167th Bde. R.F.A.	FINE DAY W.J.
Monday 20.12.15 - do -	G.O.C. R.A., 33rd Divn. rode through the village and complimented the unit on the turnout of men and horses he had seen at 3 p.m. — They belonged to No. 3 Section.	Weather dry till night. W.J.
Tuesday 21.12.15 - do -	Nothing to note. Scheme for improvement of billets sent in by 1st Battery this morning.	WET DAY W.J.
Wednesday 22.12.15 - do -	Received orders late tonight to move to vicinity of RELY on higher ground. This was no doubt the result of the [?] visit by Bri. Genl. Birch, C.R.A. 1st Corps this morning. H.Q. formed No. 3 Section. Wagon park and horse lines kept knee deep in mud.	W.J.

(73989) W.1141-463. 400,000. 9/14. H.&J.Ltd. Forms/C. 2118/10.

WAR DIARY
or
INTELLIGENCE SUMMARY.
(Erase heading not required.)

Army Form C. 2118.

Instructions regarding War Diaries and Intelligence Summaries are contained in F.S. Regs., Part II and the Staff Manual respectively. Title pages will be prepared in manuscript.

Hour, Date, Place	Summary of Events and Information	Remarks and references to Appendices
SATURDAY - 25.12.15 - LIGNY	in trenches. Men killed rather less than in BERGUETTE. This man's allowed no the Manor for an office.	W.J.
	Spent all day of frightening my Drobard horse teams. Xmas dinner in evening with toasts & tip from the Kaiser. Newspapers much appreciated.	Wind & Stormy W.J.
SUNDAY - 26.12.15 - do -	Church Service in the Schoolroom at 11.45am at which Colonel Johnson officiated in place of the Revt W.D. Graham who was reported to had to been thrown to land roads. Jaundiced by the officers men are cheerful in spite of considerable hardships caused by the weather and lack of suitable horses. But experience confirms my opinion that the present men. of so far from being ready for Active Service. A great deal of the delay on the past 5 was due to they had during - especially in N°. 2 SECTION	Stormy & stormy. W.J.
MONDAY - 27.12.15 - do -	Capt. Bore, Lieut. Frost Moore were sent to attend a Short course of instruction in supply of Ammunition with the D.A.C. of 2nd DIV. ARTY.	W.J. W.J.
TUESDAY - 28.12.15 - do -	A course of instruction in Map Reading for N.C.O. under the Co. was commenced. - Nil -	Fine day W.J.

Army Form C. 2118.

WAR DIARY
or
INTELLIGENCE SUMMARY.
(Erase heading not required.)

Instructions regarding War Diaries and Intelligence Summaries are contained in F.S. Regs., Part II and the Staff Manual respectively. Title pages will be prepared in manuscript.

Hour, Date, Place	Summary of Events and Information	Remarks and references to Appendices
WEDNESDAY - 29/12/15 - LIGNY.	Visit by B.G.C. & BLANE and Maj. Gen. H.J. LANDON. We are to have tarpaulin etc. to make shelters and to procure a pump to improve water supply which is extremely bad and scanty here.	Fine day. W.J.
THURSDAY - 30/12/15 - do -	Second party of Officers (also Phone Lines Ellipsons) Hewitt sent to 2nd D.A.C. Three wagons with 176 rounds of How'r Amm. sent to join C BATTERY 162. Bde R+A at LE QUESNOY under command of Lieut. O.E. CAUSER who is to return tomorrow.	Fine day. W.J.
FRIDAY - 31/12/15 - do -	A staff Officer arrived & say that a battalion of dismounted cavalry have arrived & were to guard here the evening. Seems our normal concentrating our billets as much as possible. The new troops began turning about 5pm. Seems the afternoon & all through the night into billets claimed for army co.	Fine in morning. Wet in afternoon. W.J.

Signed *[signature]* Lt. Col. R.J.A.

Comdg. 33rd Divl Ammunition Column

31st December, 1915.

33rd Inst.
N Pot. 2

33rd Div: Am: Col.

Army Form C. 2118.

WAR DIARY
or
INTELLIGENCE SUMMARY.
(Erase heading not required.)

Instructions regarding War Diaries and Intelligence Summaries are contained in F. S. Regs., Part II. and the Staff Manual respectively. Title pages will be prepared in manuscript.

31 JAN 1916

Hour, Date, Place	Summary of Events and Information	Remarks and references to Appendices
SATURDAY - 1st JANUARY - LINGY- LES-AIRE 1916	Supply of rations today very short. Capt. KERNAN went to BETHUNE for temporary duty with HQ. 2d. 33rd Division.	Weather windy, but not very wet. W.S.
SUNDAY - 2nd Jany - do -	The dismounted Cavalry Battalions left us early this morning. Received orders this evening to clear out of the by noon TUESDAY and go into billets at LINGHEM.	Wet & stormy day W.S.
MONDAY - 3rd Jany - do -	Sent billeting party to LINGHEM. Settling claims of LIGNY inhabitants and preparations for departure.	FINE DAY. W.S.
TUESDAY - 4th Jany - LINGHEM.	Marched to LINGHEM. 5 Kilometres. New billets inferior to those at LIGNY, but water better and more plentiful. Lost our interpreter who was ordered off by the French Mission.	Rain in afternoon W.S.

(73989) W4141-463. 400,000. 9/14. H.&J.Ltd. Forms/C. 2118/10.

Army Form C. 2118.

WAR DIARY
or
INTELLIGENCE SUMMARY.
(Erase heading not required.)

Instructions regarding War Diaries and Intelligence Summaries are contained in F.S. Regs., Part II and the Staff Manual respectively. Title pages will be prepared in manuscript.

Hour, Date, Place	Summary of Events and Information	Remarks and references to Appendices
WEDNESDAY - 5th Jany - LINGHEM.	Settling into new billets and rigging up shelters for harness.	Wet day. WS
THURSDAY - 6th Jany - do -	Nothing to note	FINE DAY. WS
FRIDAY - 7th Jany - do -	Trial march of S.A.A. wagons to see if teams can draw to call the heavier loads imposed by addition of 1200 grenades per section. Loads were 32 cwt. each for 7 S.A.A. wagons and 24 cwt. for the grenade wagons. No difficulty in drawing them. Visit by Brig. Genl. Blane.	Showery anyway day. WS
SATURDAY - 8th Jany - do -	Exchanged 4536 rounds of 18 pr. Shrapnel for an equal number of H.E. Received secret orders to be ready to entrain at 9 hours notice.	FINE morning. Wet afternoon each evening. WS
SUNDAY - 9th Jany - do -	Distributed the above H.E. Ammunition to B.A.C. Rev. Capt. GRAHAM came over from BERGUETTE and we had a church parade.	FINE DAY. WS

(7.3989) W.4141-463. 400,000. 9/14. H.&J.,Ltd. Forms/C. 2118/10.

Army Form C. 2118.

WAR DIARY
or
INTELLIGENCE SUMMARY.
(Erase heading not required.)

Instructions regarding War Diaries and Intelligence Summaries are contained in F.S. Regs., Part II and the Staff Manual respectively. Title pages will be prepared in manuscript.

Hour, Date, Place	Summary of Events and Information	Remarks and references to Appendices
MONDAY - 10th Jany - LINGHEM	Despatched a party of 10 waggons and 53 N.C.O.'s & men all told under Lt. CLUSER to hand timber at NIEPPE FOREST.	FINE DAY. WL
TUESDAY - 11th Jany - do -	Nothing particular - received further details of Nearest Entraining Scheme	Moderate & fine day WL
WEDNESDAY - 12th Jany - do -	CAPT. W.L. POWRIE received orders from G.O.C. R.A. 33rd Dvp. started for Mt. BERNENCHON this morning to take over command of 162nd Bde. Amn. Col. from CAPT. RHODES where to report & take him on the DAC. Sent to BERGUETTE for some more Obag.	FAIRLY fine day WL
THURSDAY - 13th Jany - do -	Route march for all three SECTIONS dumping ammunition Each in every to picks up. Marches of 8 to 10 miles - Capt. Powrie came back met Capt. RHODES to hand over No 2 Section kits.	Fine in morning - Sharp storm in afternoon WL
FRIDAY - 14th Jany - do	Capt POWRIE handed over No 2 SECTION to CAPT RHODES and returned to 162nd Bde A.C. at Mt. St. BERNENCHON.	MODERATE WEATHER WL

(73989) W4141-463. 400,000. 9/14. H.&J.Ltd. Forms/C. 2118/10.

Army Form C. 2118.

WAR DIARY
or
INTELLIGENCE SUMMARY.
(Erase heading not required.)

Instructions regarding War Diaries and Intelligence Summaries are contained in F. S. Regs., Part II. and the Staff Manual respectively. Title pages will be prepared in manuscript.

Hour, Date, Place	Summary of Events and Information	Remarks and references to Appendices
SATURDAY- 15th Jany- LINGHEM	ROUTE March and practice concentration of 3 Sections. about 9 miles - Pace not including one long halt 4½ miles per hour.	FINE but cold day. WS.
SUNDAY- 16th Jany -do-	DIVINE SERVICE in a field. Football in afternoon.	Moderately fine day. WS.
MONDAY- 17th Jany -do-	Horses and mules of No.1 SECTION 1st malleined on some French plan.	FINE DAY. WS.
TUESDAY- 18th Jany -do-	No 2 SECTION animals malleined. CAPT. KERNAN Returned from BÉTHUNE and Lt CAUSER and his party from NIEPPE where they are reported by the O.F.R.E.S.T Office to have done excellent work.	WET DAY. WS.
WEDNESDAY- 19th Jany -do-	Lieut. HEWITT transferred to 166th B.A.C. and replaced by 2/Lt WINBUSH from that Unit.	FINE DAY. WS.
THURSDAY- 20th Jany -do-	Nothing particular	FINE morning, Storms in afternoon. WS.
FRIDAY- 21st Jany -do-	VISIT by Genl BLANE. Making water troughs etc.	Cold, windy day. WS.

(7.3989) W4141—463. 400,000. 9/14. H.&J.Ltd. Forms/C. 2118/10.

Army Form C. 2118.

WAR DIARY
or
INTELLIGENCE SUMMARY.
(Erase heading not required.)

Instructions regarding War Diaries and Intelligence Summaries are contained in F. S. Regs., Part II. and the Staff Manual respectively. Title pages will be prepared in manuscript.

Hour, Date, Place	Summary of Events and Information	Remarks and references to Appendices
SATURDAY - 22nd Jany - LINGHEM.	Nothing particular.	WET + Windy W.J.
SUNDAY - 23rd Jany - do -	DIVINE SERVICE in field	Beautiful day W.J.
MONDAY - 24th Jany - do -	Ordered to lend 12 wagons without teams to R.F.A. Base. This means dumping a lot of ammunition and making the Column immobile.	Drizzling rain. W.J.
TUESDAY - 25th Jany - do	CINEMA and musical Entertainment for the men by Rev. Colonel BLACKBOURNE, Senior Chaplain of 1st ARMY.	FINE DAY. W.J.
WEDNESDAY - 26th Jany - do -	MARCHING ORDER parade with whole ARTILLERY of 33rd Div. for inspection by GENl. GOUGH. He did not reach us. Orders received about 9.30 p.m. to be ready to move at 2 hours notice.	FINE DAY. W.J.
THURSDAY - 27th Jany - do	Received lens wagons from Base were made all ready to move.	FINE DAY. W.J.
FRIDAY - 28th Jany - do -	Order to ~~move~~ be ready for sudden move was revoked following midnight and 1 am and revised at 5.30 p.m.	FINE DAY W.J.

Army Form C. 2118.

WAR DIARY
or
INTELLIGENCE SUMMARY.
(Erase heading not required.)

Hour, Date, Place	Summary of Events and Information	Remarks and references to Appendices
SATURDAY. 29th Jany. LINGHEM.	Standing by, ready to move at 2 hours notice. Order to stand by rendered at 11-35 p.m.	FINE DAY. W.
SUNDAY - 30th Jany - do -	Received order to take part in Divisional Manoeuvres tomorrow. Order received at 9-30 p.m. Divine Service at 9-30 a.m.	FINE DAY, but frosty. W.
MONDAY - 31st Jany - do	Took part in the manoeuvres of 12th Division - for n/a a route march of about 3½ hours	FINE DAY. W.

1st Feby 1916

[signature]
COMMANDING DIVISIONAL AMMUNITION COLUMN,
33 DIVISION

WAR DIARY
or
INTELLIGENCE SUMMARY.

(Erase heading not required.)

33rd Divisional Ar. Colum. Army Form C. 2118.

Hour, Date, Place	Summary of Events and Information	Remarks and references to Appendices
TUESDAY – 1st Feby – LINGHEM	Men bathing at the Mines at FLECHINELLE. 2nd Lieut A.W. HENLEY sent to do temporary duty with 167 B.A.C.	FINE cold day. W.d
WEDNESDAY – 2nd Feby. – do –	INTERPRETER BEAUPÈRE joined. We have been without one since 4th January.	FINE cold day. W.d
THURSDAY – 3rd Feby – do –	Nothing particular	FINE cold day. W.d
FRIDAY – 4th Feby – do	Nothing to note	FINE day after wet night. W.d
SATURDAY 5th SUNDAY 6th	Nothing to note	
MONDAY – 7 Feby – do	Lieut. Johnson proceeded for attachment to 2nd D.A.C.	WET morning. W.d
THURSDAY – 10 Feby – do –	Lt Col. JOHNSON returned from attachment to 2nd D.A.C.	FINE DAY. W.d
SUNDAY – 13th Feby – do –	Received preliminary instructions for a move to form Column Establishment	Changeable weather. W.d
MONDAY – 14th Feby – do –	Sent a party consisting of 18 N.C.O's men, 20 horses & 3 wagons complete to join 161st D.A.C. Column Establishment ordered to be reduced by these figures.	W.d

Army Form C. 2118.

WAR DIARY 33rd D.A.C.
or
INTELLIGENCE SUMMARY. Continued

(Erase heading not required.)

Instructions regarding War Diaries and Intelligence Summaries are contained in F.S. Regs., Part II. and the Staff Manual respectively. Title pages will be prepared in manuscript.

Hour, Date, Place	Summary of Events and Information	Remarks and references to Appendices
TUESDAY - 15th Feby - LINGHEM	2nd Lt. A.W. HENLEY rejoined	Very wet windy Evening. W.J.
WEDNESDAY - 16th Feby - do -	2nd Lt. MOSS went to 12th D.A.C. to learn method of bomb supply in use there.	RAIN and high wind. W.J.
THURSDAY - 17th Feby - do -	Capt. and Adjutant W. Smith went to 12th D.A.C. to see how things are done there. Warned to be ready to open detachment of D.A.C. to be attached to A + D. 167 Bde. if necessary.	FINE DAY - high wind. W.J.
SUNDAY - 20th Feby - do -	Capt. SMITH returned from 12th D.A.C.	FINE DAY W.J.
MONDAY - 21st Feby - do	Received back 12 wagons due from Bdes.	FINE DAY. W.J.
TUESDAY - 22nd Feby - do -	Nothing to note.	First Snowfall - about 2 inches W.J.
WEDNESDAY - 23rd Feby - do -	2nd Col. JOHNSON proceeded to 12th D.A.C. for temporary attachment	Cold - Frosty. W.J.
THURSDAY - 24th - do -	2nd Col. JOHNSON returned from 12th D.A.C. — Move postponed Esq'n.	Hard frost. W.J.
FRIDAY - 25th - do -	Electr wagon with teams sent to complete O.P. attachment at BEUVRY	Frost afternoon - monsoon. W.J.

(73989) W.4141—463. 400,000. 9/14. H.&J.Ltd. Forms/C. 2118/10.

Army Form C. 2118.

WAR DIARY
or
INTELLIGENCE SUMMARY.

(Erase heading not required.)

Instructions regarding War Diaries and Intelligence Summaries are contained in F.S. Regs., Part II and the Staff Manual respectively. Title pages will be prepared in manuscript.

Hour, Date, Place	Summary of Events and Information	Remarks and references to Appendices
SATURDAY - 26th July, LINGHEM.	Nothing to Note	Fine evening W.J.
SUNDAY - 27th July - do -	Nothing to Note	Decreased than W.J.
MONDAY - 28th July - do -	Packing up for move to VENDIN-LEZ-BETHUNE	Wet day W.J.
TUESDAY - 29th July. VENDIN-LEZ-BETHUNE	Marched to new billets at VENDIN-LEZ-BETHUNE. Started at 7 a.m. arrived at 11.30 a.m.	FINE DAY W.J.

H.B.Stanum Lt.Col. R.D.A.
Comdg. 33 D.A.C.

29th March 1916

(73989) W.4141-463. 400,000. 9/14. H.&J.Ltd. Forms/C. 2118/10.

Original

Army Form C. 2118.

33rd Div. Am. Column.

WAR DIARY
INTELLIGENCE SUMMARY.
(Erase heading not required.)

10th to 31st March 1916.

Instructions regarding War Diaries and Intelligence Summaries are contained in F.S. Regs., Part II. and the Staff Manual respectively. Title pages will be prepared in manuscript.

Hour, Date, Place	Summary of Events and Information	Remarks and references to Appendices
WEDNESDAY 1st March VERDIN-LEZ-BÉTHUNE	Settling down in new billets. Conference of B.A.C. Commanders.	Fine Day.
THURSDAY 2nd March	Nothing to note	Snow Rain and sleet
FRIDAY to MONDAY 3rd to 6th March		
TUESDAY 7th March	Orders received for reduction of Establishment of 59 & 60 Majors.	Sleet
WEDNESDAY 8th March	Nothing to note	Changeable
THURSDAY 9th March	Several bombs were dropped by an enemy aeroplane in fields and outskirts of the village. Three exploded but no harm done.	Snow
FRIDAY 10th March	Visit by General BLAKE, C.R.A.	Dull each day.

(73989) W.4141—463. 400,000. 9/14. H.&J.Ltd. Forms/C. 2118/10.

WAR DIARY 33 DAC
or
INTELLIGENCE SUMMARY.

Army Form C. 2118.

2nd Phase - March 1916

Hour, Date, Place	Summary of Events and Information	Remarks and references to Appendices
11th March to 19th March		
YEN DIS-LEZ-BETHUNE	Nothing to note	Fine weather
SATURDAY 18th March 1916	At 12.30 p.m. a German scout had on the Hope line at the forward head dumps today. Two of our aircraft went to recover the other. So badly that they had to be destroyed. Out of some seven aeroplanes we very slightly shelter shelter severely. They were also reported unseen as unknown. No one seems to be going over a car.	Fine duty
SUNDAY 19th March 1916	Another heavy dust making the ingles from the Gare de Mines very difficult	Fine day
20th March 1916	Nothing to note	

Army Form C. 2118.

WAR DIARY 33D.A.C.
INTELLIGENCE SUMMARY.
(Erase heading not required.)

3rd Sheet — March 1916

Hour, Date, Place	Summary of Events and Information	Remarks and references to Appendices
MONDAY 27th March VENDIN-LEZ-BETHUNE	Establishment reduced by 4 wagons complete with teams.	See 7 March 1916 W.D.
TUESDAY 28th to Friday 31st March 1916	Nothing to note.	Fine weather W.D.

2nd April 1916.

A.J. Johnson Lt. Col. R.F.A.
Commg. 33rd D.A. Ammn Column

33 DAC
Vol 5

Army Form C. 2118.

WAR DIARY 33 D.A.C.
or
INTELLIGENCE SUMMARY.
(Erase heading not required.)

Hour, Date, Place	Summary of Events and Information	Remarks and references to Appendices
SATURDAY - 1st April 1916 VENDIN-LEZ-BETHUNE	Nothing to note	Fine weather W.S.
SUNDAY - 2nd April - do	—	
MONDAY - 3rd April - do	Rev. W.D. GRAHAM C.F. left today for HAVRE BASE replacing by Rev. HEASLETT C.F.	Fine day W.S.
TUESDAY - 4th to FRIDAY - 7th -	Nothing to note	FINE but cold W.S.
SATURDAY - 8 Ap - do	CAPT. G.E. KERNAN lighter a detonator on arriving of the Rugus that he found in the mud was damaged with his hands badly - had to go to hospital.	FINE DAY W.S.
SUNDAY 9 - MONDAY 10 -	Nothing to note	Frost W.S.
TUESDAY - 11 Ap - do	2nd Lieut. F.T. GUSH left to join 166 B.A.C.	WET DAY W.S.

Army Form C. 2118.

WAR DIARY or INTELLIGENCE SUMMARY.

(Erase heading not required.)

33 D.A.C.

2nd New - April 1916

Instructions regarding War Diaries and Intelligence Summaries are contained in F.S. Regs., Part II. and the Staff Manual respectively. Title pages will be prepared in manuscript.

Hour, Date, Place	Summary of Events and Information	Remarks and references to Appendices
12th April 16. VERDINLEZ BETHUNE	Nothing to note	fine hot
13th " do		do
14th April -do-	Lieut J.J. HACQUOIL, RFA joined (temp) from Gen. Base	Dull hot
15th April -do-	Lieut A.R. MACDONALD (S.R.) joined for duty. No 20546 Driver E.H. THORNTON, No 3 Section was killed by a bullet in HARLEY St. while on duty carting bricks etc. for the Engineers	fine day hot
16th April to 21st Ap.16	Nothing to note.	Stormy hot
22nd April -do-	Lieut F.W. ELLIOTT, RFA admitted to Hospital	Wet Day
23rd April to 27th April	Nothing to note.	fine hot
28th April 16	Forwards Dumps got some verses German shells but no harm done.	fine day hot
29th & 30th April 16	Nothing to note.	hot

1st May 1916.   A.B. Johnson Lieut & Comdr R.F.A.
                        2nd Comdr 33rd D. Ammunition Column R.F.A.

Officer i/c
A.G. Office at the Base

WAR DIARY for month ending
31st May 1916 herewith

A.G. Johnson Lt Col R.A.
5 May 1916
COMMANDING DIVISIONAL AMMUNITION COLUMN,
33. DIVISION

Original

WAR DIARY
INTELLIGENCE SUMMARY.
(Erase heading not required.)

Army Form C. 2118.

33rd D.A.C.

Instructions regarding War Diaries and Intelligence Summaries are contained in F.S. Regs., Part II. and the Staff Manual respectively. Title pages will be prepared in manuscript.

Hour, Date, Place	Summary of Events and Information	Remarks and references to Appendices
Monday 1st May 1916 — VENDIN-LEZ-BETHUNE.	Nothing to note	Finis
2nd May/1916		
3rd May —	Capt. Kernan reported back to England on April 30th	Finis
4th & 5th May	Nothing to note	Finis
6th May —	Capt. Kernan and Lieut. F.W. Elliott struck off the strength of the 20th & 28th mid. respectively.	Finis day 22nd inventory
9th & 10th May	Nothing to note	Finis
11 May —	Lieut. F.W.J. Dobson joined on transfer from C.166.	Finis
12 to 21st May 1916	Nothing to note	Finis weather hot

Army Form C. 2118.

WAR DIARY
INTELLIGENCE SUMMARY
33 D.A.C.

(Erase heading not required.)

Instructions regarding War Diaries and Intelligence Summaries are contained in F.S. Regs., Part II. and the Staff Manual respectively. Title pages will be prepared in manuscript.

Hour, Date, Place	Summary of Events and Information	Remarks and references to Appendices
22nd May 1916 VENDIN-LEZ-BETHUNE	Re-organisation of the 33rd and 34th took place today. 156th, 162nd, 167th B.A.C.'s were absorbed in the D.A.C. and the latter reformed in a Headquarters and 4 Sections. 2nd Lieut. J.J. HACQUOIL, A.W. HENLEY, A.R. MACDONALD (SR) and J.W.J. COLSON were attached off; Captain D. SPURLING and J.C. ALLEN, Lieut. T.D. SHEPHERD and Lieuts. B.F. GUSH, E.G. ELLIOTT, B.E. WATERMAN, G.E.L. HANCOCK and A. MITCHELL joined.	Fine day
23rd & 24th May	Nothing to note	FINE
25th May 1916.	12 Sgt MAJORS 30 Officers 1 NCO and 53 OR sent by motor lorries to Calais - part Hammers old D.A.C.	Thunder
26th 29th May	Nothing to note	FINE
30th May	2nd Lt. J. HACQUOIL joined vice R.E.L. HANCOCK to 162 Bde	FINE
31st May BETHUNE	Headquarters of D.A.C. moved to new billets in BETHUNE	FINE

A.J. Sherman Lt Col RFA
Comdg. 33rd D.A.C.

1/6/14

Army Form C. 2118.

33rd Div: Am: Col: Vol 7 June

WAR DIARY
INTELLIGENCE SUMMARY.
(Erase heading not required.)

Hour, Date, Place	Summary of Events and Information	Remarks and references to Appendices
1st June 1916 - BETHUNE	Nothing to note	} FINE
2nd " - " -		
3rd June - " -	Lieut. W.A. ELLIOTT joined ~ posted from 157th B.A.C. R.m.	
4th to 14th June - " -	Nothing to note	Wet and stormy from 10th
15th June "	Lieut. F.W.J. COLON left ~ posted to A/167 Bde RFA	Dull and showery
16th June to 30th June 1916	Nothing to note	Wet and stormy at occasional times

1st July 1916. A J Johnson Lieut Col RFA
Comdg. 33 Divisional Amn Col

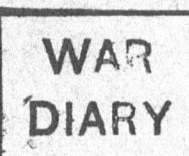

DIVISIONAL AMMUNITION COLUMN,

33rd DIVISION,

J U L Y

1 9 1 6

33 July
Army Form C. 2118.

Original

WAR DIARY
of 33 D.A.C.
INTELLIGENCE SUMMARY.
(Erase heading not required.)

Vol 8

Hour, Date, Place	Summary of Events and Information	Remarks and references to Appendices
1st July 16. BETHUNE to 5th July 1916	Nothing to note	Fine
6th July 1916. – do –	Orders received to march tomorrow night	Cloudy – emergent
7th July – do –	The Column marched into separate billets in the district between LILLERS – HINGES – BETHUNE. H.Q. and No 4 Section to CANTRAINNE No 1 to ANNEZIN, No 2 to CAUROY, No 3 & No 36 LE REVEILLON. All started between 7-8 p.m. some being the movement was a part of that of the Whole Division.	Wet till 6 p.m. then fine.
8th July – CANTRAINNE etc – do –	Rest in new billets.	
9th July – do –	H.Q. left CANTRAINNE at 12.30 p.m. and entrained at FOUQUEREUIL. No 3 & 4 Section entrained LILLERS – No 1 at FOUQUEREUIL – No 2 at CHOQUES.	Fine day

WAR DIARY 33 D.A.C.

or

INTELLIGENCE SUMMARY. July 16 — 2 sheets.

Army Form C. 2118.

(Erase heading not required.)

Instructions regarding War Diaries and Intelligence Summaries are contained in F.S. Regs., Part II. and the Staff Manual respectively. Title pages will be prepared in manuscript.

Hour, Date, Place	Summary of Events and Information	Remarks and references to Appendices
10th July.	All Sections detrained at LONG BEAU or SALEUX near AMIENS between 1 a.m. and 12 noon and marched at once to billets N.W. of AMIENS, viz:— H.Q. & No. 4 to LE MESGE — No. 2 & SOUES — No. 3 to CROUY — No. 1 to HANGEST. The Section had all been split up into quarters for the trains journey and the last detachments did not reach their billets till between 7 & 8 p.m.	Fine
11th July — LE MESGE. SOUES. CROUY. HANGEST.	Rest in billets. The Section of the Reorganized D.A.C. are being practically formed into B.A.C's as more to be expected.	Fine Day. This is a fine rolling wooded country. Sections billeted. Troops enjoy a rest.
12th July — do.	In orders received during the night one of our S.A.A. and grenade wagons (4. S. and 15 L.S.S.) to be attached to 38th D.A.C. at MEAULTE. By order of Col. A.G. off the remainder of No. 4 Section accompanied the battery in the afternoon to VECQUEMONT and CORBIE. No orders being received for H.Q. 1/DAC. though asked for — it is to stay on at LE MESGE.	Fine Day.

Army Form C. 2118.

33rd T.C.

WAR DIARY
or
INTELLIGENCE SUMMARY. July 1916 - 3rd Sheet.

(Erase heading not required.)

Instructions regarding War Diaries and Intelligence Summaries are contained in F. S. Regs., Part II. and the Staff Manual respectively. Title pages will be prepared in manuscript.

Hour, Date, Place	Summary of Events and Information	Remarks and references to Appendices
13th July 1916 - LE MESGE	H.Q. marched from LE MESGE to near TREUX about 30 miles, starting at 12.40 a.m. and arriving at 12.40 p.m. Short stay - 12 hours, including halt of 25 minutes for watering in AMIENS and one of 2½ hrs for men's breakfast & watering & feeding horses at DAOUR. Bivouacked in a wood. No casualties of any sort among horses. The other Section of the D.A.C. marched to the same place in the neighbourhood of which the 33rd DAC was assembled.	FINE.
14 July 1916 - Near TREUX	Orders received at 1 a.m. for "A" Echelon to hamess up at once for immediate move with R.F.A. BRIGADES; H.Q. & "B" Echelon to be ready to follow at 3.30 a.m. Nos 2 & 3 Sections marched towards MEAULTE between 3/3.30 am. No.1 Section stayed with 156 Bde till the middle of the day. H.Q. & B. Echelon marched at 7.35 p.m. and bivouacked at BECORDEL-BECOURT with the S.A.A. (2 Section) - No. 1 Section was with its BRIGADE	FINE.

WAR DIARY

33 D.A.C.

Army Form C. 2118.

INTELLIGENCE SUMMARY.

July 1916 — 4 Sheet

(Erase heading not required.)

Instructions regarding War Diaries and Intelligence Summaries are contained in F.S. Regs., Part II. and the Staff Manual respectively. Title pages will be prepared in manuscript.

Hour, Date, Place	Summary of Events and Information	Remarks and references to Appendices
July 15th — BECORDEL	Near MEAULTE — No 2 + 3 Sections with their new BECOURT and FRICOURT respectively. Those shell fire was furious. Whole Column assembled close to BECOURT this morning — Ammunition Dump for all sorts on N.E. side of BECOURT — no H.E. for 18 pdr. in it; had to supply from "B" Echelon. This dump transferred to FRICOURT tonight. About a dozen heavy shells fired this day. Fell a enormous lose this morning — don't within a few yards, but no damage's were done. Early this morning a Corporal and were wounded while taking up Amm to Infy Bde. This man's two very heavy to day. Our wagon broke down and has been left behind.	
January 16th — Do —	In attempting to recover the wagon left behind yesterday 4 mules were killed and one driver wounded.	Fine morning — wet later.

Army Form C. 2118.

WAR DIARY 33rd Div

INTELLIGENCE SUMMARY July 16. 5 Sheets

(Erase heading not required.)

Hour, Date, Place	Summary of Events and Information	Remarks and references to Appendices
Monday 17th – RECORDER COTTAGE	Busy day with Ammunition. New Dump/ARED working very heavily owing to publication in a review and armourer road. Lieut K.G. GUNN RAMC left for England on completion of his term of service.	FINE DAY
Tuesday 18th – do –	Nothing to note	Dull, cold day.
Wednesday 19th – do –	Very hard work for teams.	Fine day
Thursday 20th – do –	Our teams out all day. Heavy expenditure of ammn.	Fine day.
21st to 26th – do –	Nothing to note	Fine weather
30th (Sunday) – do –	Lieut J. Robt Jones in post'n from BASE. Lieut T.D. Shepherd posted to 162 Bde R7th	Fine day
Monday 31st – do –	Nothing to note	Very hot day.

A.J. Donovan Lieut. R.RA
(MMO) 33 Div Am: Column

33rd Divisional Artillery

33rd DIVISIONAL AMMUNITION COLUMN R.F.A.

AUGUST 1 9 1 6

One week

33 D.A.C.

Army Form C. 2118.

WAR DIARY
INTELLIGENCE SUMMARY.
(Erase heading not required.)

1st Res. V. A. 9

Hour, Date, Place	Summary of Events and Information	Remarks and references to Appendices
1st to 3rd August 1916. BECORDEL	Nothing to note.	Fine, hot weather.
4th August - do -	Establishment increased by 15 Gunners - 5 to each "A" Echelon Section. Auth - G.H.Q. No O.B./518 of 1st Aug. '16.	Cool - windy
5th August - do -	Lieut. E.G. ELLIOTT invalided to England on 25/July/16 - pyorrhea and shellshock.	Fine
6th to 8th August - do -	Nothing to note	Fine
9th August - do -	Lieut. I.W. CRUNIS joined on posting from 156" B.A.C. R.F.A.	Fine
10th August - do -	Nothing to note	
11th August - do -	2nd Lieut. B.E. WATERMAN transferred to Anti-Aircraft Battery 1st Army.	Fine
12th to 15th August - do -	Nothing to note	Fine, then showery

Army Form C. 2118.

WAR DIARY
33 DAC
INTELLIGENCE SUMMARY.
2 nothers.

(Erase heading not required.)

Instructions regarding War Diaries and Intelligence Summaries are contained in F. S. Regs., Part II. and the Staff Manual respectively. Title pages will be prepared in manuscript.

Hour, Date, Place	Summary of Events and Information	Remarks and references to Appendices
10th August. BECORDEL	Capt. R.D. NASMITH, R.A.M.C. joined on attachment to duty	WET.
25th to 26th August — do —	Nothing to note	FINE
27th August — do —	Lieut. A.W. HENLEY posted to 157 Bde. vice CURTIS	Wednesday
28th to 31st August. do —	Nothing to note	Though wet — don't thunder storm.

H.J. Stevenson Lt. Col. R.J.A.
Commanding 33rd British Division Column.

1st Sept. 1916.

Original
33 M.T.C.
Vol 10

Army Form C. 2118.
1st Sheet

WAR DIARY
of
INTELLIGENCE SUMMARY.
(Erase heading not required.)

Instructions regarding War Diaries and Intelligence Summaries are contained in F.S. Regs., Part II. and the Staff Manual respectively. Title pages will be prepared in manuscript.

Hour, Date, Place	Summary of Events and Information	Remarks and references to Appendices
1st to 3rd Sep. — BECORDEL	Nothing to note	Fine
4. — do —	Orders to move out of Area on 6th. received this day	Wet day
6. — do —	Marches from BECORDEL to billets at BONNAY about 9 miles. Very much delayed by traffic on road — took 4½ hours	Fine day
7 Sep. — BONNAY	Marches from BONNAY to NAOURS, about 15 miles. Time taken including one halt of 1½ hours and one of 10 minutes and about 40 minutes delay caused by traffic was 7 hours. Before starting the march 67 wagons had to be sent to CORBIE to refill with ammunition. Animals marched in fit and well. Camperparks and short water.	This day
8. — NAOURS	Marches from NAOURS to BOISBERGUE 12 miles, 4½ hours. Ample space for leaa horse-power and good water — monopoly	Fine day
9. — BOISBERGUE	Marches from BOISBERGUE to MARRISSEC and MILLY just N.E. of DOULLENS — 7 to 8 miles. 2¼ hours. Good grounds & few billets. Plentiful water	Fine day

continued —

(73989) W4141—463. 400,000. 9/14. H.&J.Ltd. Forms/C. 2118/10.

Army Form C. 2118.

WAR DIARY
of
INTELLIGENCE SUMMARY.

33rd D.A.C.

Sheet 2.

(Erase heading not required.)

Instructions regarding War Diaries and Intelligence Summaries are contained in F. S. Regs., Part II. and the Staff Manual respectively. Title pages will be prepared in manuscript.

Hour, Date, Place	Summary of Events and Information	Remarks and references to Appendices
10th Sept. — MILLY.	Marched from MILLY to LATTRE St. QUENTIN — 13 miles, 4 hours 25 minutes. Had to find Govrnmnt at NOYELLETTE 1 mile further on for N°4 SECTION and H.Q. as LATTRE was crowded. At 5 p.m. shifted N°4 Section & am away to report that lines have just been vacated by a battery with prisoners.	Foggy cloudy weather but no rain.
11th — LATTRE St. QUENTIN	No further move. Nothing to note	Dull.
12 — do —	Detached N°4 Section less 2 horse and the Artillery wagons as a S.A.A. Section to our Infantry with all S.A.A. and Grenade wagons — to GAUDIEMPRE.	Dull & Showers.
13 Aug/14 — do —	Nothing to note.	Fine — cold wind.
15 — do —	11 Bn moved from NUVELETTE to LATTRE St. QUENTIN and the 3 A.F. echelon Sections there occupied the voids vacated by 37 M.D.A.C.	Fine
16 — do —	Ordered at 2 a.m. to march at 9.45 a.m. to GAUDIEMPRE. Picking up balance of ammunition from AVESNES. Did 20 - about 10 miles in 3½ hours off which were spent in waiting outside BARLY for	

WAR DIARY
or
INTELLIGENCE SUMMARY.
(Erase heading not required.)

33 D.A.C.
3rd Sheet.

Army Form C. 2118.

Hour, Date, Place	Summary of Events and Information	Remarks and references to Appendices
	for the Ammunition wagon from AVESNES. Two Company grooms - no billets in GUDIEMPRE. In afternoon ordered to back tomorrow to place now occupied by wagon lines of two Batteries. 3rd Section has gone on to HUMBERCAMP.	Fine day
17th Sept - GUDIEMPRE	Self and Adjutant went on offer from each Batt. spent the morning reconnoitering the new villages. Marched at 1.30 pm for COUTURE &c and bivouacked there with No. 1, 2, 7+8 sections to COULLEMONT, one other Quarter was to be occupied by 26th D.A.C. - 3 miles, 1 hour. Seen 16 Ammunition wagons to batteries in front lines to deliver at night. Not enough officers for the work - Sent Mr M[?] 1 sub any ammunition, ours at dump at G.H.Q. DIEMPRE, 1 Oxd[?] all might with ammunition. 2 will be away on tomorrow and night carting R.E. Stores, 1 employed to look after Divl. Details, leaving 3 for duty with 4 sections, one for any other calls, s.a.e. for instance. This is a bad unusual state of things.	Fine day

WAR DIARY
INTELLIGENCE SUMMARY.

33 D.A.C.
by M. Reed.

(Erase heading not required.)

Army Form C. 2118.

Hour, Date, Place	Summary of Events and Information	Remarks and references to Appendices
18th Sept - COULLÉMONT.	Shifted camp to COULLÉMONT with Sections 1 and 2, leaving No 3 to go to LES ANNELLES, a farm about a mile away.	Pouring wet day.
19th Sept - COULLEMONT	Orders received to move to HENU tomorrow.	Fine day
20th - do -	Move to HENU (camp D.25 for No 4 Section) postponed till tomorrow. Order to move cancelled late by verbal message.	WET DAY
21st - do.	Received order at 3 a.m. to send No 1 & 2 Sections to LATTRE and my Section to HENU. Section marched accordingly. Orders for our H.Q. and No 3 Section to go to LATTRE on 23rd. Leaving No 4 Section in their district under VII Corps. Position will then be such that ½ a week up afterwards various march and countermarches.	Dull day, but no rain.

Army Form C. 2118.

WAR DIARY
or
INTELLIGENCE SUMMARY. 33 D.A.C.

5th Sheet

(Erase heading not required.)

Hour, Date, Place	Summary of Events and Information	Remarks and references to Appendices
23rd Sept - COULLEMONT	H.Qrs from COULLEMENT and No 3 Section from HUMBERCAMP marched into billets at LATTRE ST. QUENTIN. No 4 Sec: now attached to VII CORPS in believille, have marched from GAUDIEMPRE to RINCOURT.	Fine day.
27th Sept - LATTRE ST.QUENTIN	2nd Lieut. F.W. BEADLE and L.M. HOWARD joined on posting from 136 & 176 L Bde respectively.	Fine day
28th - 30th - do -	Nothing to note.	Fine.

AJJohnson Lt.Col R.A.
Comdg. 33rd D.A. Ammn Column

1st October 1916.

Original
33rd D.A.C.
Vol 11

WAR DIARY

INTELLIGENCE SUMMARY.
(Erase heading not required.)

1st Sheet

Army Form C. 2118.

Hour, Date, Place	Summary of Events and Information	Remarks and references to Appendices
1st October 1916 - LATTRE St. QUENTIN	Nothing to note.	Fine
2nd Oct. - do -	Orders received to move to COULLEMONT on 6th	WET
3rd Oct. - do -	Nothing to note.	WET
5th Oct. - do -	Lieut. M. A. ELLIOTT posted to 41st Div'l. Arty from 1-9-16 (Temporary)	
6th Oct. - do -	March to COULLEMONT and found 2 Sections	FINE DAY
8th Oct. - COULLEMONT	No. 4 Section marched to BAYENCOURT & bivouacked	FINE DAY
18th Oct. - do -	No. 4 Section marched from BAYENCOURT to BEAUCOURT	Wet day
19th Oct. - do -	Marched to COUIN and bivouacked there. Bad wet very wet day - horse standing - pretty good grooming for men.	Frost at night
20th Oct. - COUIN	No news of B Echelon. Got a few tents and oilcloths and made the men fairly comfortable.	Fine cold day

Army Form C. 2118.

WAR DIARY
INTELLIGENCE SUMMARY.
(Erase heading not required.)

33rd D.A.C.
2nd Rgt.

Instructions regarding War Diaries and Intelligence Summaries are contained in F. S. Regs., Part II. and the Staff Manual respectively. Title pages will be prepared in manuscript.

Hour, Date, Place	Summary of Events and Information	Remarks and references to Appendices
20th to 31st Oct - COUIN	Nothing to note	Vosges and vicinity.

1st Nov. 1916

A.J.Johnson Lieut Col R.A.
Comdg: 33rd Aust. D.A.C.

Army Form C. 2118.

WAR DIARY
or
INTELLIGENCE SUMMARY.

33rd M.A.C.

10" Sheet 5bf 12

(Erase heading not required.)

Hour, Date, Place	Summary of Events and Information	Remarks and references to Appendices
1916 1st November to ECOUVIN 11th do	Nothing to note	WJ
12th do	Lieut. E.G. ATTENBOROUGH posted and posted from 162 Bde RFA. (SUPERNUMERARY).	FINE WJ
13th do	Nothing to note.	Fine and cold WJ
do	Received warning order to march to TALMAS on 22nd inst.	WJ
22nd do	Marched (A Echelon) to TALMAS by a roundabout route - 16 miles. Very bad roads and much delayed by batteries in front and other traffic generally. Arrived at 4.45 pm.	Beautiful day WJ
23rd TALMAS	Started from TALMAS at 6.45am to march to ALLERY, a place about 11 miles S.S.E. of ABBEVILLE. At 7.5am on the road received orders to motor to BAILLEUL and BELLIFONTAINE, about 6½ miles S. of ABBEVILLE. H sent	FINE DAY WJ

WAR DIARY or INTELLIGENCE SUMMARY

33rd D.A.C. 2nd Sheet

Army Form C. 2118.

Hour, Date, Place	Summary of Events and Information	Remarks and references to Appendices
1916		
25th Nov. - BELLIFONTAINE	Head of Column reached BELLIFONTAINE at 4.55 p.m. via FLIXCOURT and L'ETOILE - 23 miles - including halts 3 hours + 25 minutes + 10 minutes + 1 hr. 50 mins. trots & can + 4 minutes stopped at Railway Crossing + 10 minutes. (Total 3 hr. 50 min). The last wagon of rear Section passed through BELLIFONTAINE at 5 pm. having been longer delayed at CONDÉ Rly Crossing.	W
26th Nov - BELLIFONTAINE	Orders received to march to New Billets Re 26" - H.Qrs. I + III Sections to ALLERY, No 2 Section to BETTENCOURT.	Very warm day W
26 Nov. - do -	No 2 Section marched to BETTENCOURT at 9.15 am via BELLIFONTAINE and SORIEL. HQr and Nos I and III Sections at 9.30 am. to ALLERY via GRANDSART and HALLENCOURT - 5 miles	FINE + cooler W

WAR DIARY Army Form C. 2118.
or
INTELLIGENCE SUMMARY.
(Erase heading not required.)

33rd D.A.C.
2nd Sheet

Hour, Date, Place	Summary of Events and Information	Remarks and references to Appendices
1916 NOVEMBER 27th ALLERY	Visit by Major Genl. PINNEY, G.O.C. 33rd Divn. Received warning order to be prepared to move into FORWARD AREA about Dec 8th by march route.	FINE DAY.
28th 30th ALLERY	Nothing to note.	FINE

1°December 1916

W. Lumley pat R.F.A.
for O.C. 33 D.A.C.

Army Form C. 2118.

WAR DIARY
INTELLIGENCE SUMMARY.

B Echelon 33rd D.A.C.
1st Then

(Erase heading not required.)

Place	Date	Hour	Summary of Events and Information	Remarks and references to Appendices
CARNOY	8.XI.16	12.30p	Movement of B Echelon 33rd DAC from Operation Area to Billet at DAOURS via MEAULTE, VILLE, MERRICOURT, LA-NEUVILLE. Head of column not to pass through VILLE till 2 pm. (Map. ALBERT Combined Sheet)	33rd Divr. S.403 of 7/11
DAOURS	9.XI.16	12 noon	March by road from DAOURS to ARGOEUVES via AMIENS to Billet.	
ARGOEUVES	10.XI.16	9 am	March by road from to Rest Billet at E RONDELLE via PICQUIGNY, HANGEST, LONGPRE. (Map AMIENS 1/100,000 and ABBEVILLE 14 (1/100,000))	

1st December

[signature] Capt R.F.A.
for OC B Echelon 33 DAC

Army Form C. 2118.

WAR DIARY
INTELLIGENCE SUMMARY.
(Erase heading not required.)

33rd D.T.C. Vol 13

Hour, Date, Place	Summary of Events and Information	Remarks and references to Appendices
December 1916		
In the Field 1st & 2nd	Nothing to note	Fine Weather
3rd	Orders received for No. 2 Section to be prepared to march into Forward Area on 5th inst. Baptism Bone admitted to hospital with Bronchitis.	Fine weather
4th	Nothing to note	
5th	No. 2 Section marched from BETTENCOURT at 8 AM en route for BRAY-SUR-SOMME via PICQUIGNY and AILLY-SUR-SOMME to billet on night 5th/6th at ST. SAUVEUR. Orders received for H.Q. & No. 1 Section to march by same route on 9th inst. No. 3 Section to remain at ALLERY until further orders	
6th & 7th	Nothing to note	
8th	H.Qrs only marched to billets in ST. SAUVEUR en route to front near BRAY about 13 miles.	Fine Weather
9th	H.Qrs marched to VAUX, No. 1 Section to ST. SAUVEUR. No. 3 remaining at ALLERY	Foggy & wet.
10th	H.Qrs marched to Camp 14, 2 miles W. of BRAY - about 6 miles. No. 1 Sec to VAUX	Wet-day
11th	No. 2 Section marched from Camp 14 to a camp about 1½ miles N.E. of BRAY on MARICOURT Road. No. 1 Section marched to Camp 14.	Fine morning, wet afternoon
12th	H.Qrs. & No.1 Section followed No.2 Section into Camp – a very bad mc. no shelter & a sea of mud – 600 yards from a road. The last wagon of the 1st did not get in till 8 p.m.	Wet day
13th	Lieut E.Y. Warburgh evacuated sick to England Robinack off strength	Mild dull day
14th	Captain H. Freeman joined us posting to No. 1 Section	Dull & showery
15th	Nothing to note	wet day
16th	2nd Lt E.Y. Warburgh rejoined from Base & taken on strength	wet day
17th, 18th, 19th, 20th		Frost fast night - Clear morning. Wind rain & Snow later. Fog on 17th, dull 18th, Freezing 19th & 20th.
21st	Nothing reported in No. 3 Section	Wet day

Army Form C. 2118.

WAR DIARY
INTELLIGENCE SUMMARY.
(Erase heading not required.)

Instructions regarding War Diaries and Intelligence Summaries are contained in F. S. Regs., Part II. and the Staff Manual respectively. Title pages will be prepared in manuscript.

Hour, Date, Place	Summary of Events and Information	Remarks and references to Appendices
December 1916		
22nd	Moved into dug outs near by.	Wet day
23rd	Nothing to note	Wet + high wind
24th	Several German shells fell in & around camp, but no harm done	Fine day
25th, 26th, 27th	Nothing to note	Changeable weather
28th	Lt Col A.S. Dunlop (Army 40th D.A.C. arrived to take over Command of the two D.A.C's on relief of H Qrs	Fine day, but foggy
29th	Lt. S.S. Attenborough slightly, & Sgt Bowles severely wounded by shell bursting between them. Both thrown off their horses, they were taking up ammunition to guns	Wet day
30th	Captain H. Freeman posted with effect from 14th inst.	Heavy rain last night - showers during day.
31st	Nothing to note	Mild + Showery.

1 Jan/17 A.J.Sturgeon
Lt Col.
Comg 47 3rd D.A.C.

Duplicate ~~Original~~

Army Form C. 2118.

33rd D.A.C.

Vol 1st Sheet

WAR DIARY
or
INTELLIGENCE SUMMARY.
(Erase heading not required.)

Instructions regarding War Diaries and Intelligence Summaries are contained in F. S. Regs., Part II. and the Staff Manual respectively. Title pages will be prepared in manuscript.

Hour, Date, Place	Summary of Events and Information	Remarks and references to Appendices
1917		
TUESDAY BRAY-SUR-SOMME 2nd January	Marched from camp at 10.15 am with HQ and "A" Section to D.A.C. for VAUX-S-SOMME on way to Rest Area. At 11.30 am passed No W.2 Section B Eche. and 3 of their B Echelon at B Echelon 33rd D.A.C. and 3 of B Echelon 40th D.A.C. arrived at VAUX at 1.15 pm and found no billets available, all being already occupied by 156th & 175th Bdes RFA and a battery of 4th Div. So I altered my orders and sent back, first for horses — most of 2nd Line on man. The men bivouaced in a shed. Any field now remnant dream of the wagons.	FINE day
WEDNESDAY VAUX-S-SOMME 3rd January	Marched to LONGPRE HALT 15 miles W of AMIENS. 16 miles. I hour watering 1½ hours halt. Fed billets near Longpre.	FINE day but cold and windy

(73989) W4141—463. 400,000. 9/14. H.&J.Ltd. Forms/C. 2118/10.

Army Form C. 2118.

WAR DIARY 33rd DAC
or
INTELLIGENCE SUMMARY.
(Erase heading not required.)

2nd Sheet

Instructions regarding War Diaries and Intelligence Summaries are contained in F. S. Regs., Part II. and the Staff Manual respectively. Title pages will be prepared in manuscript.

Hour, Date, Place	Summary of Events and Information	Remarks and references to Appendices
1917		
THURSDAY 4th January LONGPRÉ HALT	Marched into rest billets at CONDÉ. No 4 Sec 33 DAC to LONGPRÉ clear by ambulances. Snow reducing 1½ hour halt.	Very wintry. Fine evening.
	Capt. H BONE marched to ENGLAND via strength of Strength with Effect from 30.12.16	
SUNDAY 7th January CONDÉ	Scheme recent up reorganization of Artillery in general and DAC in particular.	Fine even day
S 8 to 14 January CONDÉ	Nothing to note	
15th January	No 4 Section marched up to LONGPRÉ HALTE on route for firing line.	Dull day - frost last night
16th January	2nd Lieut S W WILLETT and G BARTHOLOMEW posted and joined from BASE	Frost at night. Dull day.

Army Form C. 2118.

WAR DIARY
or
INTELLIGENCE SUMMARY
(Erase heading not required.)

33rd D.A.C.
3rd New

Instructions regarding War Diaries and Intelligence Summaries are contained in F.S. Regs., Part II. and the Staff Manual respectively. Title pages will be prepared in manuscript.

Hour, Date, Place	Summary of Events and Information	Remarks and references to Appendices
1917		
FRIDAY, 19th January 1917	Marched to ST SAUVEUR 11 miles, met the 2 Section of 8th DAC	FINE DAY
SATURDAY, 20th January	Marched with 2 Section 8 DAC to Camp XII near BRAY - 22 miles. Started 8.40 am, arrived at 5.15 pm - delayed by long column on front and later by slippery roads.	FINE cold day
SUNDAY, 21st January	At Camp XII	FINE cold day
MONDAY, 22nd January (CAMP XII)	Remained at Camp XII but in consequence of orders to get nearer to R.F.A. sections made arrangements to move to VAUX E. of SUZANNE (known as)	Frost & snow.
TUESDAY, 23rd January VAUX (East of SUZANNE)	Marched to billets at VAUX - 5½ miles. 3 hours. Next Section from Camp north of BRAY to LA NEUVILLE. South of BRAY	FINE FROSTY DAY
24th to 28th January 1917	Nothing to note	Frost frosty
29th January - 1917	2.I.C. BARTHOLOMEW posted to 162nd Bde R.F.A.	frost frosty

HQ JThomas Lieut Col RFA
Comdg 33rd Div Amm Colum

1st Feby 1917

Army Form C. 2118.

B. Echelon
33 DAC

WAR DIARY
or
INTELLIGENCE SUMMARY.
(Erase heading not required.)

Instructions regarding War Diaries and Intelligence Summaries are contained in F. S. Regs., Part II. and the Staff Manual respectively. Title pages will be prepared in manuscript.

Place	Date	Hour	Summary of Events and Information	Remarks and references to Appendices
L16.B. BRAY.	1-1-17	8.30a	Movement of B.Echelon 33rd D.A.C. from L16B to Camp 114 (K.23.A) Starting point for march to Rest Area No 6. (ALBERT. Combined Sheet.).	33rd Brigade Arty Order No 72 (Tucea?) fca
Camp 114.	2-1-17	11.30am	March by road to Billet at VAUX-SUR-SOMME.	fca
VAUX.	3-1-17	10 am	March by road to Billet at LONGPRÉ. HALT. (AMIENS)	fca 33rd D.A.
LONGPRE HALT.	4-1-17	9.45am	March by road to Billet at LONGPRÉ-SUR-SAINT, destination in No. 6 AREA.	B.M.1123/1. fca 4-1-17.
			MAP Sheets AMIENS & ABBEVILLE.	
LONGPRE-S.SAINT	15-1-17	-	Movement from Rest Area to relieve 17th FRENCH Div. March by road to ARGOEUVES	Table 'A' 33rd B.A. fcd Swn No 256.6
ARGOEUVES	16-1-17		March by road to Billets at VAUX & SAILLY-LE-SEC.	K.A.
VAUX.	17-1-17	-	March under orders of 19th Inf. Bde to Camp 112. (19th Inf. Bde Order No 188.	fca
CAMP 112	19-1-17	.	Movement to temporary camp at L10.6 and commencement of supply of munitions to Main Div'l Ammn Dump at HEM. (H8.a.5.8) System of Supply:- Rail Head to Main Div. Ammn Dump, then Orders D.A.C.Dump by LORRY 15th Corps Park; G.S Wagon from D.A.C Dump to HEM. Main Div Dump; Water by Pack Mule and PETROL from 33rd Div by Inf Transport to Right and Left Bde Dumps.	Administrator fca 33rd Divn WD/17/A
L.10.6.	23-1-17	6.30a	Movement to No 3 Camp LA NEUVILLE (L38.A) and D.A.C. Dump established. Weather very frosty, but travelling good by road.	fca

A.J. Plowny Lt Col R.T.A.
Commg 33rd DAC Column (?)

DUPLICATE

WAR DIARY
or
INTELLIGENCE SUMMARY.
(Erase heading not required.)

33rd BAC   Army Form C. 2118.
1st Then.
Vol 15

Hour, Date, Place	Summary of Events and Information	Remarks and references to Appendices
February 1917		
7. VAUX.	H.Q.R. marched to new billets in outskirts of BRAY	Very cold and windy WS
14. BRAY sur Somme	A+B Section (men and vehicles only) were brought to BRAY from ALLERY by train & camp of 162nd BAC RFA. Rest of A+B Sevans and horses and Horses by tramp of 33rd BAC — 30 miles. The Section is to be broken up and the vehicles among the sections of 33rd BAC and the chief of them of III Div — XI Corps	Fine and moderate cold WS
	1st T RWR and a detachment from 5th Section III Div transferred to 5th BAC by Orders V Corps	Mild wet sunny WS
	2nd tr. from A.3 debar conveying from 7-1914 and the war on the land of living art tassion and ins Louis & 36th BAC III CORPS	Mild + fine WS

WAR DIARY Army Form C. 2118.

33rd D.T.R.C.

or

INTELLIGENCE SUMMARY. 2nd Sheet

(Erase heading not required.)

Hour, Date, Place	Summary of Events and Information	Remarks and references to Appendices
February 1917 - continued		
22nd BRAY-on-SOMME	Disposal of No 3 Section party consisting of 6-150m drum wagons and one 6T motor with team & water complete, sent to III CORPS. Capt D SPURLING assumes command. No 4 Section becomes No 3 Section.	Von/70/91 N.S. Canteeny N.S.
23rd - do -	No 2 Section moved from Camps on MARICOURT Road to Camp No 3, LA NEUVILLE (BRAY) Capt D SPURLING posted to III A.T.A.C.	From army list
25th - do -	Lieut F.W.T. MAGGOOL posted to 42 Coy 31st to take over Transport Duties but Thence to No 273.	From army list

Myfather FWW R.D.
Commander 33rd B.T.C.

Army Form C. 2118.

33rd D.A.C.

1st Sheet Vol/6

WAR DIARY
of
INTELLIGENCE SUMMARY.
(Erase heading not required.)

Instructions regarding War Diaries and Intelligence Summaries are contained in F.S. Regs., Part II. and the Staff Manual respectively. Title pages will be prepared in manuscript.

Hour, Date, Place	Summary of Events and Information	Remarks and references to Appendices

1917.

1st to 10th MARCH — BRAY — Nothing to note.

11th March — BRAY — Horses taken to shelter owing to snow storm.

12th to BREBIÈRES — [illegible]

25th March — [illegible] to La Motte-Brebière at work

26th March — NAOURS — [illegible]

27th March — NAOURS — [illegible] Beauval-Rivière —

Army Form C. 2118.

33rd D.A.C.
2nd Sheet

WAR DIARY
or
INTELLIGENCE SUMMARY.
(Erase heading not required.)

Instructions regarding War Diaries and Intelligence Summaries are contained in F.S. Regs., Part II and the Staff Manual respectively. Title pages will be prepared in manuscript.

Hour, Date, Place	Summary of Events and Information	Remarks and references to Appendices
1917		
25th March — BEAUVAL–RIVIÈRE	Marched to HONVAL near FRÉVENT via Auxi-sous-le-Château, Boubigny & trains by troops	Fine day
29th March — HONVAL	Marched to HABARCQ 2 miles west of ARRAS via Mont Sorrel, to entrain troops there	Mild no rain
30th March — HABARCQ	Nothing to note	[illegible]
	10 April 1917	HyG Hoare Lt Col comdg 33 D.A.C.

Original

Army Form C. 2118.

WAR DIARY 33rd D.A.C.
INTELLIGENCE SUMMARY.
(Erase heading not required.)

1st sheet.

Instructions regarding War Diaries and Intelligence Summaries are contained in F.S. Regs., Part II. and the Staff Manual respectively. Title pages will be prepared in manuscript.

Hour, Date, Place	Summary of Events and Information	Remarks and references to Appendices
1917 1st/2nd/3rd April — HABARCQ	Nothing to note.	JF EASTERLY WINDS. SNOW AND RAIN.
4th April — DUISANS	Marched into Camp at DUISANS - 3½ miles. Only 30 tents to be had for 434 all ranks. No news yet of No 3 Section who are still with the Infantry and still organised as a S.A.A. SECTION.	WET AND COLD.
6th April —	Two inches of snow fell on our camp about 8 p.m. but no damage.	WET.
9th April — ARRAS	Marched to Camp about ½ N.W. of BAUDIMONT GATE of ARRAS. Started 8.40 p.m. and took 6½ hours to do the 3 mile march owing to roads being blocked by traffic. Last vehicle was not in till 3.30 a.m. on the 10th.	Changeable weather — Several snow and rain showers during night.

(7.3989) W4141—463. 400,000. 9/14. H.&J.Ltd. Forms/C. 2118/10.

Army Form C. 2118.

WAR DIARY 33rd D.A.C.
or
INTELLIGENCE SUMMARY. 2nd sheet

(Erase heading not required.)

Instructions regarding War Diaries and Intelligence
Summaries are contained in F. S. Regs., Part II.
and the Staff Manual respectively. Title pages
will be prepared in manuscript.

Hour, Date, Place	Summary of Events and Information	Remarks and references to Appendices
1917		
TUESDAY - 10th April. ARRAS	Warned to be ready to move at short notice but eventually remained in same camp.	Coln moved, W to N. - many heavy snowstorms. Wet cold on 19th
TUESDAY - 17th April. ARRAS	No 970252 Driver S. Peachy No 2 Sec. killed in action	
16.30 ARRAS	Working to rest	Fine.

1st May 1917.

A.J. Johnson Lt Col. R.F.A.
Comdg. 33rd British Column

(73989) W.1141—463. 400,000. 9/14. H.&J.Ltd. Forms/C. 2118/10.

Army Form C. 2118.

WAR DIARY
33rd D.A.C.
INTELLIGENCE SUMMARY.
(Erase heading not required.)

Instructions regarding War Diaries and Intelligence Summaries are contained in F. S. Regs., Part II and the Staff Manual respectively. Title pages will be prepared in manuscript.

Hour, Date, Place	Summary of Events and Information	Remarks and references to Appendices
TUESDAY – 1st May – 6. 3 p.m. may. ARRAS	Nothing to note	FINE. WS.
FRIDAY – 4th May – ARRAS	A big dump of Artillery Amm. and S.A.A. etc. belonging to the 15th Div. took fire and was completely destroyed between 5 am and midnight. It was within 300 yards of ammunition dumps of ours which however remained safe though many fragments and spent bullets shells fell in and about it. The N.C.O. i/c No. 20390 Corporal T. NIGHTINGALE showed courage and coolness in remaining on duty in remaining by the dump all night.	FINE. NS
5th to 9th May –	Nothing to note	FINE generally — some rain. NS
10th May –	Changed Camp to the E. side of ARRAS on DOUAI Road. Fine ground and watertrough.	FINE. NS. Continued.

Army Form C. 2118.

WAR DIARY
33rd D.A.C.
INTELLIGENCE SUMMARY.
Gun sheet.
(Erase heading not required.)

Instructions regarding War Diaries and Intelligence Summaries are contained in F. S. Regs., Part II. and the Staff Manual respectively. Title pages will be prepared in manuscript.

Hour, Date, Place	Summary of Events and Information	Remarks and references to Appendices
1917		
11th May — ARRAS.	No. 20510. Driver H. FISHER, No. 3 Section, killed in action. 5 others wounded by the same shell.	FINE weather. W.L.
12th to 25th May —	Nothing to note	Fine W.L.
26th May —	Capt. F.C. PACKHAM and Lieut. C. MOORE posted and joined from BASE	FINE W.L.
27th to 31st May	Nothing to note.	FINE W.L.

A.J. Johnson
Lieut. Col. R.A.
Comdg. 33 D.A.C.

1st June 1917.

33 D Am Col
Vol 19

WAR DIARY
or
INTELLIGENCE SUMMARY.
(Erase heading not required.)

Army Form C. 2118.

Hour, Date, Place	Summary of Events and Information	Remarks and references to Appendices
In the Field 1.6.17	Nothing to note. Fine day.	
" 2.6.17 to 11.6.17	Nothing to note. Fine weather.	
" 12.6.17	Several shells fell in our neighbourhood during the morning. Just after 9 a.m. one fell on the building containing No.1 Section; office & store, killing Corporal W.W. Preston and slightly wounding 5 other men. From a fragment of the base of the shell appeared to be of 15" cal. Fine day.	
" 13.6.17 and 14.6.17	Nothing to note. Fine weather.	
" 15.6.17	2nd Lieut. V.W. CUNIS posted to 162nd Brigade " F.W. BEADLE " 156th " LIEUT. T.P. LYSAGHT " from 156th " 2nd LIEUT. F.C. ROSE " " 162nd "	
" 16.6.17	CAPTAIN J.C. ALLEN under orders from Divisional Artillery joined 156th Brigade for instruction in gunnery &c. CAPTAIN F.C. PACKHAM posted temporarily to command of No.3 Section from att. No 1 Section.	
" 17.6.17 to 20.6.17	Nothing to note.	
" 21.6.17	Marched to camp at BOIRY-ST.MARTIN - about 7 miles. Two hours due S. of ARRAS. Fine morning. Thunderstorm in evening.	
" 22.6.17 to 30.6.17	Nothing to note. Mostly fine weather. Captain J.C. ALLEN returned from attachment to 156 Brigade & resumed command of No.3 Section on 25th inst.	

RJ Stenson Lt Col
Com 33 D.A.C.
1 July 14

Original
Copy

33rd D.A.C. Army Form C. 2118.
Vol 20 Sheet

WAR DIARY
INTELLIGENCE SUMMARY.
(Erase heading not required.)

Instructions regarding War Diaries and Intelligence Summaries are contained in F.S. Regs., Part II and the Staff Manual respectively. Title pages will be prepared in manuscript.

1917 Hour, Date, Place	Summary of Events and Information	Remarks and references to Appendices
July		
TUESDAY - 3rd - BORRY-ST-RICTRUDE	Captain W.L. POWRIE left on transfer (probation) to 24th BASE PARK Coy. R.E. at ROUEN.	FINE
MONDAY - 16th - do -	Captain R.D. NASMYTH, R.A.M.C. left to ENGLAND on termination of engagement. Captain H.M. DRAKE, R.A.M.C. joined from 19th Field Ambulance.	FINE
SUNDAY - 22nd - do -	R.A. Divisional SPORTS at which the D.A.C. did very well, as also at the HORSE SHOW a few days ago.	FINE
MONDAY - 23rd - do -	Marched with "A" Echelon to ORVILLE - behind the 162nd and 156th Brigades R.F.A. - 18 miles; 6 hours including halts amounting to 1 hour. Soon found our billets.	FINE

Continues

WAR DIARY
or
INTELLIGENCE SUMMARY.
(Erase heading not required.)

Army Form C. 2118.

33rd D.A.C.

2nd Sheet

Hour, Date, Place	Summary of Events and Information	Remarks and references to Appendices
1917 JULY. TUESDAY, 24th - ORVILLE	The D.A.C. was broken up into 13 detachments for transport by train. Entrained at DOULLENS and AUTHIEULE and detrained at DUNKERQUE and ADINKERKE next day.	To: X 15
WEDNESDAY - 25th DUNKERQUE	After detraining at DUNKERQUE the main body of Nº 1 and 2 Sections and H.Q. marched to Camp at FERME du NORD, SOUTH of UXEM, about 12 miles, arriving there between noon and 3.30 p.m. They were followed at 8 p.m. and midnight by two Sections of "B" ECHELON. The 3rd detachment of Nº 1 Section that had accompanied the latter of "B" ECHELON never accompanied about midnight. "B" de also rejoined never Capt. PACKHAM. Nº1 Section of "B" ECHELON. detrained at ADINKERKE and marched to billets at COXYDE-BAINS.	Hexagram in the morning, but fine in the afternoon Continues

Army Form C. 2118.

WAR DIARY
INTELLIGENCE SUMMARY.

33rd D.A.C.

2nd Sheet

(Erase heading not required.)

Hour, Date, Place	Summary of Events and Information	Remarks and references to Appendices
1917 JULY. THURSDAY - 26th FERME-du-NORD	The 1st detachment of Nº 2 SECTION rejoins from GHYVELDE at 3 p.m. Nº 3 SECTION (⅔ of it) under Capt: ALLEN marches for COXYDE	FINE - COOL.
TUESDAY - 31st	- do - Marched to COXYDE-BAINS and camped in the dunes, the place itself being shelled by the enemy. Distance 15 miles. Time 5½ hours enclosing halts. The whole D.A.C. re-united at this place.	Dull day, but no rain till 10 p.m.

1st August 1915

MJ Johnson Col. R.H.
Comdg. 33 D.A.C.

Original

WAR DIARY

33rd D.A.C.

Army Form C. 2118.

INTELLIGENCE SUMMARY.

(Erase heading not required.)

Instructions regarding War Diaries and Intelligence Summaries are contained in F.S. Regs., Part II. and the Staff Manual respectively. Title pages will be prepared in manuscript.

1917 Hour, Date, Place	Summary of Events and Information	Remarks and references to Appendices
Aug 1917 Sunday 5th COXYDE-BAINS	Rev. G.H. HEASLETT C.F. re-attached on rejoining from sick leave	Fine
Saturday 11th do	H/Q B/- and B. Echelon shelled pretty continuously by a gun (and a few rounds from a howitzer) between 10.30 p.m. and 4.30 a.m. – One man hit, 18 animals killed and about 6/45 killed about 18 wounded.	Stormy
Sunday 12th do	Capt H.M. DRAKE R.A.M.C. to 1st Brigade Rgr – replaced by Capt. J.K. SMALL R.A.M.C. from 1st Brigade. Changed Camp owing to the shelling last night. New Camp just north of the fork of the LA PANNE - COXYDE road to PANNE - FURNES roads.	FINE

WAR DIARY 33rd D.A.C. Army Form C. 2118.
or
INTELLIGENCE SUMMARY. 2nd Sheet
(Erase heading not required.)

Hour, Date, Place	Summary of Events and Information	Remarks and references to Appendices
1917 August cont.d		
Wednesday 22nd In Parc	Lieut. S.W. WILLETT attached temporarily to C/162 Bde.	Stormy
Thursday 23rd - do -	A new War Establishment received - W.O. 642 as W.O.(S.D.2) 4th August 1917.	Tuesday Stormy night
Saturday 25th - do -	No 20768 Bomb.dr A. Young No 3 Section struck off for whilst in charge of wagon No NIEUPORT. Notification of grant of Military Medal to No 20500 Serg.t W. KILLIAN No 2 Sec for gallantry on 14th in.	FINE
Sunday 26th - do -	No 93848 A. (a/s) W. HOOKER No 6 Sec. Posted when in charge of pack mule carrying ammn to 152 Bde.	Storm in night
27th to 31st - do -	Nothing know.	Stormy

[signature]
Comm.g 33 D.A.C.

"Original"

Army Form C. 2118.

33 D.A.C.

Vol 2 1st Sheet

HEADQUARTERS,
33RD
WAR DIARY
or
INTELLIGENCE SUMMARY.
(Erase heading not required.)

Instructions regarding War Diaries and Intelligence Summaries are contained in F. S. Regs., Part II. and the Staff Manual respectively. Title pages will be prepared in manuscript.

Hour, Date, Place	Summary of Events and Information	Remarks and references to Appendices
1917		
SUNDAY – 2nd Sep – LA PANNE	The D.A.C. marched to LES MOERES, S.W. of ADINKERKE – 9 miles, 2½ hours.	FINE
MONDAY – 3 Sep – LES MOERES	Marched to WEMAERS-CAPPELL W. of CASSEL. 19 miles – 6 hours marching time.	FINE
TUESDAY – 4 Sep – WEMAERS – CAPPELL	Marched to Camp at RENINGHELST, S.E.of POPERINGHE, passing round N. of CASSEL via OUDEZEELE	FINE
TUESDAY – 11 Sep – RENINGHELST	2/Lt. C.R. HENZELL attached from 152 Brig R.FA.	
WEDNESDAY – 12 Sep – do –	Lieut. H.E. BENSON, U.S. Med. Reserve Corps replaced Capt. J.K. SMALL R.A.M.C. in medical charge of Column	FINE
MONDAY – 17 Sep – do –	The Commanding Officer, Lieut. Col. A.G. JOHNSON and Capt. H. RHODES Commg No 2 Section killed in action – shrapnel. Interred at RENINGHELST MILITARY CEMETERY.	FINE

(73989) W4141–463. 400,000. 9/14. H.&J.Ltd. Forms/C. 2118/10.

Army Form C. 2118.

WAR DIARY
or
INTELLIGENCE SUMMARY. 33 D.A.C.
2nd Sheet

(Erase heading not required.)

Instructions regarding War Diaries and Intelligence Summaries are contained in F.S. Regs., Part II and the Staff Manual respectively. Title pages will be prepared in manuscript.

Hour, Date, Place	Summary of Events and Information	Remarks and references to Appendices
1917		
TUESDAY. 18th Sept. RENINGHELST	20217 Driver J.W. STONE, No 2 Sec. died of wounds received in action on 17th inst.	FINE
WEDNESDAY. 19th do_	Lieut. C. MOORE rejoins from duty with 33rd DEPOT BATTALION and appointed temporarily No. 2 Section vice Capt. RHODES to the Command of	FINE
THURSDAY. 20th do	20900 Driver W.M. SCRANNEY No 2 Sec. killed in action. One man wounded and one animal killed.	FINE
SATURDAY. 22nd do.	20372 DRIVER E. STONE, No 2 Sec. died of wounds received in action on 20th inst.	FINE
SUNDAY. 23rd do	59625 Dr. BARBER. A. No 4 Sec. killed in action.	FINE
MONDAY. 24th do.	2/Lt E.T. WINBUSH killed in action whilst attached to C/162 Bart. 17676 Gr. H. GREEN No 2 Sec. killed in action	FINE
TUESDAY. 25th _do_	2/Lt A.H. WHITING wounded in action whilst attached to D/162 Bae... HQ and No 1 Sub Section moved to new camp at about 1 mile S.W. of DICKEBUSCH	FINE

(839) W.4141—463. 400,000. 9/14. H.&J.I.Ltd. Forms/C. 2118/10.

Army Form C. 2118.

WAR DIARY
of 33 D.A.C.
INTELLIGENCE SUMMARY.
3rd Sheet
(Erase heading not required.)

Instructions regarding War Diaries and Intelligence Summaries are contained in F.S. Regs., Part II and the Staff Manual respectively. Title pages will be prepared in manuscript.

Hour, Date, Place	Summary of Events and Information	Remarks and references to Appendices
1917 September.		
WEDNESDAY. 26th DICKEBUSCH (Nun)	2/Lt A.R. MACDONALD and C.R. HENZELL attached to 156 Bde and Lt L.M. HOWARD attached to 162 Bde.	FINE
SUNDAY. 30th - do -	Lt. F.C. ROSE and 31 n.c.o's gunner attached to 162 Bde and a similar number of O.R. to 156 Bde. No.43910 Dr. S.J. Anford N° 1 Section killed in action. Casualties in action 28th inst.	FINE
	Casualties during September 1917 —	
	3 Officers killed 1 " wounded 4 O.R. killed 11 " " wounded (incl. 2 accidental)	

W. Turnbull Capt. R.F.A.
Comdg: 33 D.A.C.

10th October 1917.

33 DAC

Army Form C. 2118.

WO 95/93

WAR DIARY
or
INTELLIGENCE SUMMARY.
(Erase heading not required.)

Instructions regarding War Diaries and Intelligence Summaries are contained in F.S. Regs., Part II. and the Staff Manual respectively. Title pages will be prepared in manuscript.

Hour, Date, Place	Summary of Events and Information	Remarks and references to Appendices
In the Field 1st October 1917	Nothing to note.	
" 2nd "	Horse lines bombed from enemy aeroplanes at 10.15 P.M. - 21 animals killed and destroyed, 12 wounded.	
" 3rd "	69 N.C.O.'s when posted to batteries to replace casualties. Lieut. T.P. LYSAGHT posted to B/162 Bde.	
" 11th to 16th "	Nothing to note.	
" 17th "	No 71010 Corpl B. FOX, No 2 Section awarded Military Medal for gallantry on 19.9.17	
" 18th "	Nothing to note.	
" 19th "	Colonel L. FORDE C.M.G. assumed Command of DAC. Posted from 18th Corps 5th Army.	
" 20th "	No 22360 Driver J. Palmer, No 2 Section killed in action	
" 21st "	Nothing to note.	
" 22nd "	No 11684 Sgt A.H. ELLIOTT No I Section wounded in action. Struck off Strength	
" 23rd "	2/Lieut. A.J. MINSON joined from C/193 Army Bde on 20/10/17 and posted to No. 1 Section	
" 24th "	2/Lieuts. S. CORK and W.R. WOODCOCK joined from BASE.	
" 25th "	Nothing to note.	
" 26th "	FRENCH INTERPRETER MALLETT withdrawn from Column by FRENCH MISSION 33rd Div	
" 27th & 28th "	Nothing to note.	
" 29th "	Lieut. W.E. HYATT joined from BASE - posted to No. 3 Section	
" 30th "	Nothing to note.	
" 31st "	Horse lines bombed night 31st Oct/1st Nov - 5 horses killed, 11 wounded. No. L/46666 a/Bom. J. SALMON, No. 1 Section wounded in action.	

H Carver 26.ON.A.
Lt. Colonel RA, Commanding 33rd DAC

Original

Confidential 16

Army Form C. 2118.

33rd D.A.C.

WAR DIARY
INTELLIGENCE SUMMARY.
(Erase heading not required.)

Instructions regarding War Diaries and Intelligence Summaries are contained in F.S. Regs., Part II. and the Staff Manual respectively. Title pages will be prepared in manuscript.

1st Sheet

9/5/24

1917 Hour, Date, Place	Summary of Events and Information	Remarks and references to Appendices
NOVEMBER.		
SATURDAY 3rd HUBERTSHOEK near DICKEBUSCH	Orders received to march on 4th inst 5th h.t. neighbourhood of WALLON CAPPEL. 2nd Lieut. W.H. KERR joined from BASE & reported to N°1 SECTION	
SUNDAY 4th -do-	N°1 Section marched to REST AREA and billeted at HOUCK, near CASSEL.	
MONDAY 5th -do-	H.Qrs and N°2 Section marched to REST AREA. 20 miles. H.Q. billets in BAVINCHOVE — N°2 Sec. at MULSE HOUCK. 2nd Lieuts. A.R. MACDONALD and L.M. HOWARD posted to 156 Brigade and 162 Brigade respectively.	
TUESDAY 6th BAVINCHOVE near CASSEL	Lieut. A.J. MINSON posted to D/156 Bde R.F.A.	
THURSDAY 8th -do-	2nd Lieut. F.C. ROSE posted to D/162 Bde R.F.A.	

Army Form C. 2118.

WAR DIARY
INTELLIGENCE SUMMARY.
(Erase heading not required.)

33rd D.A.C.   2nd Sheet

Hour, Date, Place	Summary of Events and Information	Remarks and references to Appendices
November 1917		
SUNDAY-11th- BAVINCHOVE	Orders received to march tomorrow to BOUVELINGHEM.	
MONDAY-12th- -do-	Marched to new REST AREA near BOUVELINGHAM. H.Q. billeted in HAUT LOQUIN - No. 1 and 2 SECTIONS at REBERGUES. 25 miles.	
THURSDAY-15th HAUT LOQUIN	Lieut. C.R. BURRIDGE (Res. Cav.) left from attachment for A.S.C. Depot (H.T.†S.) HAVRE.	
	Casualties in action during the month. } Nil.	

1st DECEMBER 1917. J Forbes Colonel
Comdg. 33 D.A.C.

Army Form C. 2118.

WAR DIARY
or
INTELLIGENCE SUMMARY.
(Erase heading not required.)

33rd D.A.C.

"1st" SHEET.

Instructions regarding War Diaries and Intelligence Summaries are contained in F.S. Regs., Part II. and the Staff Manual respectively. Title pages will be prepared in manuscript.

Hour, Date, Place	Summary of Events and Information	Remarks and references to Appendices
1917 DECEMBER		
SATURDAY - 1st HAUT LOQUIN	Orders received to march on 2nd inst to ZERMEZEELE en route for front line. Captain F.C. PACKHAM rejoined from attachment to R.H. & R.F.A. BASE DEPÔT.	
SUNDAY - 2nd - do -	H.Q. and N°s 1 and 2 SECTIONS marched at 8.45 A.M. to WEMAERS CAPPEL, near CASSEL, and billeted therefor the night. Head of column arrived 9.15 p.m.	Very cold - Snow squalls in evening.
MONDAY 3rd WEMAER CAPPEL	Continued march to neighbourhood of VLAMERTINGHE W. of YPRES - arrived 3.45 p.m.	
SATURDAY - 8th VLAMERTINGHE	REORGANIZATION of the Column carried out in conformity with War Establishments, Pt VIIA, N° 642 dated 4th March 1917. N°3 SECTION (B.Echelon) became S.A.A. SECTION. All personnel and animals rendered surplus by this	

Army Form C. 2118.

33rd K.B.A.C.
2nd Sheet

WAR DIARY
or
INTELLIGENCE SUMMARY.
(Erase heading not required.)

Instructions regarding War Diaries and Intelligence Summaries are contained in F.S. Regs., Part II and the Staff Manual respectively. Title pages will be prepared in manuscript.

Hour, Date, Place	Summary of Events and Information	Remarks and references to Appendices
1917		
DECEMBER (continues)	Reorganisation as absorbed into Divisional Artillery. Vehicle harness and saddlery sent to BASE.	
SUNDAY - 23rd VLAMERTINGHE	No 2 and No 7 A.A. SECTIONS moved to new camps situated about a mile S.E. of POPERINGHE.	
THURSDAY - 27th — do —	H.Q. and No 7 SECTION moved to new camps alongside No 2 SECTION.	
SATURDAY - 29th POPERINGHE	Lieut. C.P. HENZELL left to join H.Q. R.F.C. as probationary OBSERVER.	
SUNDAY 30th — do —	2nd Lieut. L.C. HOPKINS (S.R.) joined from BASE and posted to S.A.A. SECTION.	

J. Forde Colonel
Comdg. 33rd K.B.A.C.

1st January 1917.

Original
Army Form C. 2118.

Confidential

WAR DIARY
or
INTELLIGENCE SUMMARY.
(Erase heading not required.)

33rd D.A.C.

1st SHEET

Vol 26

Instructions regarding War Diaries and Intelligence Summaries are contained in F.S. Regs., Part II. and the Staff Manual respectively. Title pages will be prepared in manuscript.

Hour, Date, Place	Summary of Events and Information	Remarks and references to Appendices
1918. JANUARY.		
1st to 8th — BUSSEBOOM Near POPERINGHE	Nothing to note.	
9 — VLAMERTINGHE	H.Q.s and M.T. and S.A.A. Section moved to Camps about ½ mile S. of VLAMERTINGHE — N°2 SECTION to 1 mile E of POPERINGHE	
16th — do —	2/Lt. A. MITCHELL left for ENGLAND, having been allowed to resign his commission to resume medical studies	
17 — do —	1st Lieut. H.O. MALDINER, U.S.M.R. joined from 99th D.A.C. Ambulance for attachment as med. Officer.	
21st — do —	CAPT. G.B. MACTAVISH R.A.M.C. left for 99th F.A. on relief by 1st Lt. MALDINER.	

Army Form C. 2118.

33rd D.A.C.
2nd Sheet

WAR DIARY
or
INTELLIGENCE SUMMARY
(Erase heading not required.)

Instructions regarding War Diaries and Intelligence Summaries are contained in F.S. Regs., Part II. and the Staff Manual respectively. Title pages will be prepared in manuscript.

Hour, Date, Place	Summary of Events and Information	Remarks and references to Appendices
JANUARY - 1918		
22nd VLAMERTINGHE	2/Lt E. KIRKMAN joined from BASE - posted to N°2 Section	
30 -	On march to Column marched at 7 am on via Hitchcroft 4th Army Rest Area. Night in OUDEZEELE AREA.	
31st - do -	Left OUDEZEELE 8 am and marched to SERQUES N of ST. OMER and billeted there for the night. Casualties during month - NIL.	

2nd February 1918.

W. Smithfield. R.J.A.
Commanding 33 D.A.C.

Army Form C. 2118.

WAR DIARY
INTELLIGENCE SUMMARY.
(Erase heading not required.)

33rd D.A.C.

1st SHEET.

Instructions regarding War Diaries and Intelligence Summaries are contained in F.S. Regs., Part II. and the Staff Manual respectively. Title pages will be prepared in manuscript.

Hour, Date, Place		Summary of Events and Information	Remarks and references to Appendices
1918 February			
1st	MERCK ST. LIEVIN	Marched from SERQUES at 8 a.m. and arrived at MERCK ST. LIEVIN in the THIEMBRONNE area at 2 p.m.	
8th	— do —	Lieut. R.S. CREED (T) joined from BASE and posted to S.A.A. SECTION.	
16th	— do —	Lieut. L. HARKNETT posted to N°.1 SECTION from B/152 Bde. R.F.A. Lieut. S. ATTENBOROUGH to N°.2 SECTION from A/162 Bde. R.F.A.	
19th	— do —	N°.1 SECTION marched to WAVRANS	
20th	— do —	H.Q., N°.2 SECTION and S.A.A. SECTION marched to neighbourhood of RENESCURE, being joined by N°.1 SECTION at WIZERNES.	
21st	RENESCURE	Continued march and billeted at WAEMAERS CAPPEL	
22nd	VLAMERTINGHE	Marched to Camps in the neighbourhood of VLAMERTINGHE N°.1 SECTION to 1½ miles E. of POPERINGHE	
		Casualties in action during the month — NIL.	

1st March 1918

J. Forde Colonel
Comdg. 33 D.A.C.

ORIGINAL

Original

Army Form C. 2118.

WAR DIARY
or
INTELLIGENCE SUMMARY.

33rd Divisional Ammunition Column

(Erase heading not required.)

Hour, Date, Place	Summary of Events and Information	Remarks and references to Appendices
MARCH, 1918.		
VLAMERTINGHE.		
SATURDAY, MARCH 2.	Captain R.W. BARCLAY, 2nd Life Guards joined for attachment as HORSE MASTER.	
SUNDAY, MARCH 24.	2/Lt. L. HARKNETT posted to 5th Army from No.1 Section.	
SUNDAY, MARCH 31.	20705 Driver HALES, C, S.A.A. Section wounded in action.	

J. Stott Colonel,
cmdg. 33rd. D.A.C.

33rd Divisional Artillery.

33rd DIVISIONAL AMMUNITION COLUMN R.F.A.

APRIL 1918.

Original
Confidential

Army Form C. 2118.
33 D.A.C.
1st SHEET.

WAR DIARY
INTELLIGENCE SUMMARY.
(Erase heading not required.)

Hour, Date, Place	Summary of Events and Information	Remarks and references to Appendices
April 1918		
1st VLAMERTINGHE	Warning order received for S.A.A. Section to move with the Division (2nd Artillery) on 5th April.	
7th -do-	S.A.A. Section entrained at POPERINGHE under orders direct from H.Q. 33rd Div. — Destination unknown.	
8th -do-	No. 1 Section ordered to move the same day from their camp in C.4 (Sh.28) to No 2 Camp, PESSELHOEK (A.20.d.1.1.) Sh/28.	
10th -do-	Orders received at 11 a.m. for No. I and II Sections to march at 3 p.m. to positions BAILLEUL and NEUVE EGLISE — No. I Sec. to take orders from the commanding OC 156 Bde R.F.A. and No. 2 Sec under No. 1 of No. 162 Bde R.F.A. H.Q. instructions to move with one of the Sections, marched with No. 1 and billetted for the night in CORPS LAUNDRY, DRANOUTRE. No. 1 S.C. opens War DRANOUTRE at 11.45 p.m. Letters received to await orders.	

Original

Army Form C. 2118.

WAR DIARY of 33rd DAC

INTELLIGENCE SUMMARY
2nd Sheet
(Erase heading not required.)

Instructions regarding War Diaries and Intelligence Summaries are contained in F.S. Regs., Part II. and the Staff Manual respectively. Title pages will be prepared in manuscript.

Hour, Date, Place	Summary of Events and Information	Remarks and references to Appendices
11th DRANOUTRE	No 2 Section marched to DRANOUTRE and camped in M.3.d.5.3 (Sh/28).	
	H.Qrs. Camp Shelled from 10 a.m. to 12.30 p.m. – no Casualties. Marched at 2 p.m. for LEEDS Camp, E.of LOCRE. Inspecting N.1 Sec. have left there for WESTOUTRE. Forward ammunition Park established KOKEREELE Camp (R.17.b.5.3 Sh/27) they being now attached to 9. DAC.	
12th KOKEREELE Camp WESTOUTRE	No 1 Section sent an available gunners (17) to 112 Bde R.F.A. in compliance with order of V.C. Brigade. No 2 Section marched to new camp at M.17.c.4.7 (Sh/28) Canada Corner	
14th	No 7 Sec ordered to new position about 1 mile N. of WESTOUTRE in L.35 (Sh/27).	
15th	H.Qrs. joins No 1 Sec.	
16th CANADA CORNER	No. 2 Section moved to new position at G.15.4.2.6 Sh 28.	
18th RENINGHELST	No 2 Section moved to new camp at RENINGHELST (G.35.d.6 Sh.28)	

Original

Army Form C. 2118.

WAR DIARY
of
INTELLIGENCE SUMMARY.
(Erase heading not required.)

33 D.A.C.
3rd Fleet.

Instructions regarding War Diaries and Intelligence Summaries are contained in F. S. Regs., Part II and the Staff Manual respectively. Title pages will be prepared in manuscript.

Hour, Date, Place	Summary of Events and Information	Remarks and references to Appendices
19th HOUTKERQUE	H.Qrs 9 Non Sec moved to New Camp 3/4 m NW of HOUTKERQUE (L.24.a.sh/27).	
20th RENINGHELST	No 2 Sec. came under the orders of O.C. 9th D.A.C. in relief to 9th Div.	
25th POPERINGHE (1 m. N. of)	HQ 9 & 3 Section moved to new position — H.Qrs to L.10 central L.17.b. .2. to L.7.a. (Sheet 27)	
26th - do -	O.C. 9th D.A.C. instructed SECTIONS that ammn. would be brought their zone by lorry and that D.A.C. wagon lines to allow ammn. to batteries wagon lines only instead of to battery positions.	
30th - do -	2/Lt. E. KIRKMAN, No 2 Sec. left to join 122 D.A.C. R.F.A. in accordance with telegraphic memo from C.R.A. 33rd Div.	
	Casualties during month — Officers — Nil Other Ranks — Killed in action — 3 Wounded — 29 (2 at duty) Horses Killed — 17.	

2nd May 1918   [signature] Colonel
                Commdg. 33 D.A.C.

Original.

Army Form C. 2118.

33rd D.A.C.

JC 30

WAR DIARY
INTELLIGENCE SUMMARY
(Erase heading not required.)

Instructions regarding War Diaries and Intelligence Summaries are contained in F.S. Regs., Part II and the Staff Manual respectively. Title pages will be prepared in manuscript.

Hour, Date, Place	Summary of Events and Information	Remarks and references to Appendices
	MAY - 1918	
SATURDAY 4th - POPERINGHE (1 mile west of) - 27/L.10 central.	1st Lieut. H.O. MALDINER, U.S.A. M.O.R.C. to 156 Bde. R.F.A. for duty. (Capt.) H.M. DRAKE, R.A.M.C. joined from 156 Bde. R.F.A. for attachment.	Auth. A.D.M.S. 33rd Div. No. M/21/187 dy. 2/5/18
SUNDAY 5th - do -	No. 1 SECTION moved to WINNEZEELE into ARMY RESERVE.	
	Lieut. W.G. HYATT and 2nd/Lt. R. SCREED posted from S.A.A. SECTION to No. 1 and II SECTIONS respectively. 2/Lt. O.E. CAUSER from No. 1 SEC. and 2/Lt. G.F. GRUSH from No. 2 SEC. posted to S.A.A. SECTION.	
FRIDAY 10th - do -	No. 2 SECTION moved to WINNEZEELE into ARMY RESERVE. Army relieved in action by No. 1 SECTION from ARMY RESERVE.	
SUNDAY 12th - do -	2/Lt. R.S. CREED No. 2 SECTION posted to 162 Bde. R.F.A.	
MONDAY 13th - do -	Lt. (T/Capt.) H. FREEMAN, Comg No. 1 SECTION and 2/Lt. R.E.W. McDONALD (S.R.) (attached from 156 Bde R.F.A.) admitted to hospital (sick).	
WEDNESDAY 15th - do -	2/Lt. R.E.W. McDONALD (S.R.) (ex hospital) posted from 156 Bde R.F.A.	

Army Form C. 2118.

33rd D.A.C.

2nd Sheet

WAR DIARY
or
INTELLIGENCE SUMMARY.
(Erase heading not required.)

Instructions regarding War Diaries and Intelligence Summaries are contained in F.S. Regs., Part II. and the Staff Manual respectively. Title pages will be prepared in manuscript.

Hour, Date, Place	Summary of Events and Information	Remarks and references to Appendices
	MAY - 1918.	
SATURDAY 18th PROVEN (Map S.W. 4)	H.Q. and No 1 SECTION from W. of POPERINGHE and No 2 SECTION from WINNEZEELE moved to new Camps about 1 mile S.W. of PROVEN into ARMY RESERVE.	
SUNDAY 19th - do -	2/Lieut. E.W. BOTTOM (S.R) and W.T.C. EKINS (S.R) joined from BASE and posted to No 2. SECTION.	
MONDAY 20th - do -	REPRESENTATIVE Detachments of the Units of the Division reviewed by the COMMANDER II ARMY. The D.A.C. Detachment consisting of 3 Officers and 24 O.R. (Capt. J.C. ALLEN in command). 2nd/Lieut. L.C. HOPKINS (S.R) S.A.A. SECTION transferred to 2nd Army A.A. Group with effect from 13th May 1918.	
MONDAY 27th - do -	2/Lt. E.W. BOTTOM (S.R.) admitted to hospital (accidental injury). Casualties during month - NIL.	

in action
Stowe Colonel
Comdg 33 D.A.C.

1st June 1918

Original

Army Form C. 2118
1st Sheet

S.A.A. SECTION (attached)
33 D.A.C.

WAR DIARY
or
INTELLIGENCE SUMMARY.
(Erase heading not required.)

Instructions regarding War Diaries and Intelligence Summaries are contained in F.S. Regs., Part II. and the Staff Manual respectively. Title pages will be prepared in manuscript.

Place	Date	Hour	Summary of Events and Information	Remarks and references to Appendices
STAPLE.	1-5-18	2 pm	Movement of SAA Section 33rd DAC from STAPLE Area to WARDRECQUES Area. Route STAPLE 33B/S15b - 27/T·11·C. RENESCURE - LE·PONT·DE·CAMPAGNE - 36ᵃ/A5D. and A·11·C.	Order 302 of 1/5/18.
BANDRINGHEM	2·5·18		Movement of 33rd Bn., Personnel by road from BLARINGHEM area (from VIII Corps (2nd Army Reserve) to XXII Corps area and will be in XXII Corps Reserve.	33rd Arty Order no. 303 of 2-5-1918
" "	3·5·18	9 am	SAA Section DAC by road with 100R by 18de Group to 27/K15+16. Route. CAMPAGNE.CH. PONT·DE·CAMPAGNE — RENESCURE — 27/T·10·C. LONGUE-CROIX — ST MARIE CAPPEL — TERDEGHEM — STEENVOORDE 100⁴/ᵇʸ 18de Sheet 36ᵃ and 27 K/50,000. Billet at K15·D·82.	Order 337 2-5-1918
27/K15·D·82	4·5·18	7 am	Movement to Wgd. at 27/L14·B·87. Ammunition Dump taken over at 28/G·13D·7·. Ammunition Supply from Dump to Infantry Bde Transport in BRANDHOEK and OUDERDEM areas by SAA Section thence by Inf: Transport to by in line at DICKEBUSCH.	
27/L14·C·87	9-5-18	2 pm	Movement to 33rd Bn³ Area at 27/K18·6·9·6.	
" "	5·5·18		One Officer posted to No1 Section 33rd DAC. One to No2 Sec. 33 DAC. One from No2. One Officer posted from No1 " " " " " "	

Horace Colome
Comndg 33rd DAC

1 June 1918

"Confidential" "Original"

33rd D.A.C.
1st Sheet.

Army Form C. 2118.

WAR DIARY
or
INTELLIGENCE SUMMARY.
(Erase heading not required.)

WO 31

Instructions regarding War Diaries and Intelligence Summaries are contained in F.S. Regs., Part II. and the Staff Manual respectively. Title pages will be prepared in manuscript.

Hour, Date, Place	Summary of Events and Information	Remarks and references to Appendices
	JUNE, 1918	
THURSDAY 6th PROVEN (M.S.W.4)	Moved into action from Army Reserve and reoccupied Camps as follows :- H.Q. in 27/L.13.b.5.o.- N°1 Sec. 27/L.14.d.#11a - N°2 Sec. on 27/L.10.c.82. S.A.A. Section Horsanway 27/K.18.b.9.6. Ammunition Refilling Point at 25/G.4. b.3.4. - Supply mostly by Light Railway direct to battery positions.	
FRIDAY 4th ABEELE (about 1 km N.W.) (27/L.13.b.5.0.)	D.A.M. Captain H. FREEMAN in Command of N°1 Sec. evacuated sick to ENGLAND, and struck off the strength with effect from 10th inst. T/Capt. F.H. WARR, M.C. posted from 162 B.A.C. to command N°1 S.C. vice FREEMAN, with effect from 12th inst.	
SUNDAY 16th — do —	2/L. R.E.W. McDONALD evacuated to England, sick, and struck off the strength with effect from 14th inst.	
SUNDAY 23rd — do —	2/L. E.W. BOTTOM, (S.R) evacuated to U.K., sick, and struck off the strength with effect from 13th inst.	

Continued -

WAR DIARY or INTELLIGENCE SUMMARY

33rd D.A.C.

Army Form C. 2118.

2nd Sheet.

Hour, Date, Place	Summary of Events and Information	Remarks and references to Appendices
MONDAY 24th — do —	CAPT. C. de C. PELLIER R.A.M.C. joined for duty from 101st F.A. in relief of Capt. H.M. DRAKE R.A.M.C. to 19th BDE.	Auth: A.D.M.S. 33rd Div. N-24.6.18.
FRIDAY 28th — do —	ESTABLISHMENT. The items of all Q.F. Ammunition wagons of Nos. 1 & 2 Sections reduced from 6 animals to 4. Spare animals increased from 10 to 16, and spare animals from 20 to 32 per Section. The net reduction on the Establishment of each Section being 18 drivers and 36 animals. Capt. — BLAKIE R.A.M.C. joined on 27th from 19th H.Q.A. in relief of (Acting Capt.) PELLIER R.A.M.C. to 4 O.E. Div. Lieut. H.B. EMERSON, U.S.A. M.O.R.C. joined from 99th F.A. in relief of Capt. — BLAKIE R.A.M.C.	Auth: A.D.M.S. 33rd Div. M/21/201 d. 26/6/18

J.D. [signature]
Colonel
Comdg. 33rd D.A.C., R.F.A.

2nd July 1918.

Original

Confidential

Army Form C. 2118.

33rd D.A.C.

O.M. Kiel

Vol 32

WAR DIARY
or
INTELLIGENCE SUMMARY.
(Erase heading not required.)

Hour, Date, Place	Summary of Events and Information	Remarks and references to Appendices
	JULY 1918	
1/4 mile N. of ABEELE (29/L.13.b.50)		
WEDNESDAY 3rd	H.Q. and No.1 SECTION moved to new camp about 2 miles N. of POPERINGHE — (27/F.18.a.35 and F.17.b.6.3 respectively).	
SATURDAY 6th	No.2 SECTION moved from 27/L.10.c. to camp at 28/A.20.c.73. Casualties in action O.R. 2 (including 1 returning at duty)	

Appendix 1918
J Jones
Colonel
Comdg. 33rd D.A.C. R.F.A.

Original

Army Form C. 2118.

WAR DIARY
or
INTELLIGENCE SUMMARY
(Erase heading not required.)

33 D.A.C.

Confidential

Instructions regarding War Diaries and Intelligence Summaries are contained in F.S. Regs., Part II. and the Staff Manual respectively. Title pages will be prepared in manuscript.

Hour, Date, Place	Summary of Events and Information	Remarks and references to Appendices
	August 1918	
TUESDAY 26th POPERINGHE (1m North)	S.A.A. SECTION marched from 27/K.18 & 9.6. under orders direct from 33rd Division	SECTION'S DIARY attached.
Tuesday. 27. - do -	Lt. M.T. SWEENEY, M.O.R.C., U.S.A., joined from 16th K.R.R.C. For medical duty in relief of Lt. EMERSON, M.O.R.C., U.S.A., to 16th K.R.R.C.	
THURSDAY 29. - do -	H.Qrs and Sections 1 and 2 marched to HAEN DEKOT Area near PROVEN on relief in line by 66th D.A.C.	
SATURDAY 31st PROVEN (Area)	Details received into Column as PROVEN, our neighbourhood this night and morning of 1st Sept — in 11 trains — to PREVENT neighbourhood to join Third Army. Casualties in action during month — 1 O.R. wounded.	

J. Jones
Lt. Col.
Commdg. 33 D.A.C.
31st August 1918.

Confidential
Original

Army Form C. 2118.

33 D.A.C.

Vol 1 Sheet 1

WAR DIARY
INTELLIGENCE SUMMARY
(Erase heading not required.)

Hour, Date, Place	Summary of Events and Information	Remarks and references to Appendices
	SEPTEMBER, 1918.	
SUNDAY, 1st CANETTEMONT (near FREVENT)	H.Q. No 1 and 2 Sections detrained at BOUQUEMAISON, PETIT HOUVIN and FREVENT respectively during the night.	
MONDAY, 2nd	10 1/2 a.m. unit marched to CANETTEMONT, where all were billeted.	
SATURDAY, 14th LOUVENCOURT	Marched from CANETTEMONT at 8.30 p.m. for LOUVENCOURT en route for THIRD ARMY AREA. Arrived 6 a.m. 15th and are this billeted in village.	
SUNDAY, 15th BEAULENCOURT	Marched at 8.15 p.m. for BEAULENCOURT - 3 m. S.E. of BAPAUME.	
MONDAY, 16th BEAULENCOURT	Arrived 6 a.m. Marched at 4 p.m. for ST MARTINS WOOD - about midway between SAILLISEL and MANANCOURT. Joined 5th CORPS and attached to 17th Div.	
TUESDAY, 17th ST MARTIN'S WOOD	Formed A.R.P. at Sh 57c/V.9.b.8.8. for supply of ammn to First Artillery Brigades, viz:- 157th and 162nd of 33 D.A. and 3rd and 122nd Army F.A. Brigades.	

To SHEET 2.

WAR DIARY

33 DAC

Army Form C. 2118.

INTELLIGENCE SUMMARY
(Erase heading not required.)

3rd Sheet

Instructions regarding War Diaries and Intelligence Summaries are contained in F.S. Regs, Part II. and the Staff Manual respectively. Title pages will be prepared in manuscript.

Place	Date	Hour	Summary of Events and Information	Remarks and references to Appendices
FREVENT	28.8.18	6.30am	Entrainment at FREVENT and march route to Billets at MILLY.	33rd Bisn Q/15/1/66 (R Section SAA 33 DAC) of (L Section SAA 33rd Dac) 26.8.1918.
	29.8.18	9.30am	" " " " " "	
			(Sheet Sens No. 11)	
MILLY	15.9.18	6.15pm	Move of 33rd Bisn to V Corps Area. All moves by night. SAA Section 33rd DAC by march route to billets at ACHEUX via HALLOY - THIEVRES - AUTHIE - IVB - LES-ARTOIS.	33rd Bisn Order No. 345 9.14.7.18
ACHEUX	16.9.18	5.30pm	March route of SAA Section 33rd DAC to BAZENTIN-LE-GRAND via ALBERT. (CONTALMAISON - LONGUEVAL - G (Sheet Sens 11 and (57C 1-40,000)	Y 98/1/806 (Verbal Order 9/15/5/8)
BAZENTIN LE GRAND	18.9.18	5am	Movement of SAA Section 33rd DAC to LE-TRANSLOY in support of Operations of 21st Bisn f.C.A. of 33rd Bisn Sheet 57C 1-40,000	Verbal Order f.C.A. of 33rd Bisn
LE TRANSLOY	20.9.18	8am	Movement to Villa 99 and taking over of munition Dumps at MANANCOURT and HEUDECOURT from 91st Bisn. Personnel at MANANCOURT DUMP 1 NCO 2 men, HEUDECOURT Dump (W21.6.22) 1 NCO 6 men with 1 Officer 1 NCO + 3 ORs (Bombers from infantry). (Sheet 57C - 1-40,000	33rd Bisn N°B/17/142 9/15/5/8 f.C.6
Villa Q.99	27.9.18	2am	3 L.G.S wagons destroyed in supply of ammunition to 33rd Bisn T. Morten Batteries near PEIZIERE (Sheet 57C-1-40,000	f.C.6

JC Allen Capt. R.n.
Comdg S.A.A. Sec 33rd D.A.C.

WAR DIARY or INTELLIGENCE SUMMARY

Army Form C. 2118.

Original

Place	Date	Hour	Summary of Events and Information	Remarks and references to Appendices
				33 (British)
2/K 18.96	20.8.18		Move of 33rd Division (less Artillery) by Tactical Train. Personnel and selected Transport by Rail, remainder by March Route.	Div Order N23&04 17/8 /Ca
— do —	20.8.18 12:45 am		March of SAA Section 33rd Div Ammn Column by road from 2/K18.96 to 100K/15/62 WORMHOULT "A" AREA. Billet night 20 & 21st Aug. 18. at ZEGGERS-CAPPEL (Ref Sheet 27.) Transports of 100K Brigade Groups to follow WATOU — HOUTKERQUE — HERZEELE Route;— Order No 367 6/18/B /Ca 8 Transports of 100K Brigade Groups on 20th and 21st Aug. 18 to be commanded by Captain J. C. Allen.	
ZEGGERS-CAPPEL	21.8.18	9 am	March of S.A.A. Section 33rd D.A.C. by road to WATTEN and EPERLECQUES AREAS ROUTE. ERKELSBRUGGE — BOLLEZEELE — MERCKEGHEM — WATTEN to Billet at EST. MONT. (HAZEBROUCK Sheet.).	No — /Ca
EST-MONT.	26.8.18		33rd (British) Div (less Artillery) to be prepared to move by Strategical Train at any time after 6 am August 24th 18. to another Army.	33rd Division GS/4189/36.5 /Ca
EST-MONT.	27.8.18	6 pm	½ S.A.A Section 33rd D.A.C. march to WIZERNES for entrainment by 1.4 am 28th	33rd Division no 2/157/66 /Ca
— ,, —	28.8.18	1 pm	½ SAA — ,, — 33rd DAC march to WIZERNES for entrainment by 7.4 pm 28th Entrain HAZEBROUCK 54 and LENS 11. Entrain LE-GOUICH — IVERGNY AREA (Sheet and march to Billets at LE-GOUICH — IVERGNY AREA (Sheet 36/8-18.	/Ca
EST MONT	27.8.18	5 am	33 (British) Divn (less Artillery) will be transferred from Second Army to Third Army where it will be held in 33rd (B) Divn Orders GHQ Reserve and will be administered by XVII Corps.	/Ca N2343 & 27-8-18

27-8-1918. Comdg S.A.A. Section 33rd D.A.C. J. Allen Capt R.F.A.

Army Form C. 2118.

33rd D.A.C.

2nd Sheet

WAR DIARY or INTELLIGENCE SUMMARY

(Erase heading not required.)

Instructions regarding War Diaries and Intelligence Summaries are contained in F.S. Regs., Part II. and the Staff Manual respectively. Title pages will be prepared in manuscript.

Hour, Date, Place	Summary of Events and Information	Remarks and references to Appendices
	SEPTEMBER 1918	
SUNDAY, 22nd - ST. MARTIN'S WOOD	Ceased to be attached to 17th Div.	
SATURDAY, 28th - MANANCOURT	Moved to new camp to E. of CANAL DU NORD, opposite MANANCOURT.	
SUNDAY, 29th - do -	All Q.F. Ammn. Wagons with teams and personnel, of Nos. 1 & 2 Sections ordered to join batteries, wagon lines. G.S. Wagons of these Sections brigaded with H.Q. of Column.	
MONDAY, 30 - HEUDICOURT	Moved to W.14.a/cd 57t - between FINS and HEUDICOURT. Battle Casualties during month — 2 O.R. wounded. 7 animals killed by enemy shellfire.	

1st October 1918. By Lonmg. 33 D.A.C.
W. Smith, Capt. R.F.A.

TO SHEET 3

3/3

Army Form C. 2118.

33rd D.A.C.

Vol. 35

WAR DIARY
or
INTELLIGENCE SUMMARY.
(Erase heading not required.)

Instructions regarding War Diaries and Intelligence Summaries are contained in F. S. Regs., Part II. and the Staff Manual respectively. Title pages will be prepared in manuscript.

Hour, Date, Place	Summary of Events and Information	Remarks and references to Appendices
Oct 6th Sunday	Marched to X.11.c.28. (54) W. of HONNECOURT. attached 38th Div.	
" 7th Monday	Lieut B.A. FOYLE. (T.F.) joined from BASE and reported to D.Q. Station	
" 9th Wednesday	Ceased to be attached to 38th Div. moved to E. of ESCAULT and bivouaced at S.14.a.5.8. E. of LA TERRIERE.	
" 10th Thursday	Marched to CLARY, and established A.R.P. at P.5 & a.5. BERTRY. Lieut (54 B)	
" 23rd Wednesday	Marched to TROISVILLE. P.5. a.5.8. arrived 5,30 a.m. Lieut(54 8)	
" 24th Thursday	marched to MONTAY. K.23. a.6.4. arrived 6 am and attached to 38th Division. Lieut(51B)	
	One soldier during march 15 O.R. wounded and 157 horses killed	

J Stone
Col. Comdg.
33 Divisional A.C.

Original

33rd D.A.C.

Army Form C. 2118.

1st Sheet

WAR DIARY
INTELLIGENCE SUMMARY
(Erase heading not required.)

Instructions regarding War Diaries and Intelligence Summaries are contained in F.S. Regs., Part II. and the Staff Manual respectively. Title pages will be prepared in manuscript.

Hour, Date, Place	Summary of Events and Information	Remarks and references to Appendices
	November, 1918	
5th MONTAY	Marched to ENGLEFONTAINE.	
6th ENGLEFONTAINE	Marched to LE GRAND PATURE.	
7th LE GRAND PATURE	Marched to SARBARAS at 16 hours - arrived 23 hours. Distance about 17 miles. Seven kinds of blocks.	
11th SARBARAS	Hostilities ceased at 11.0 hours.	
12th -do-	All R.F. Ammunition Wagons with teams and personnel which had been attached to batteries since 29th Sept. last - rejoined the Column.	
14th -do-	The Column less S.A.A. Section, marched to new billets at CROIX.	To green sheet.

Army Form C. 2118.

33rd D.A.C.

2nd Sheet

WAR DIARY
or
INTELLIGENCE SUMMARY.
(Erase heading not required.)

Instructions regarding War Diaries and Intelligence Summaries are contained in F.S. Regs., Part II. and the Staff Manual respectively. Title pages will be prepared in manuscript.

Hour, Date, Place		Summary of Events and Information	Remarks and references to Appendices
15th	CROIX	November 1918 continued. Westward march continued to CLARY.	
16th	CLARY		
18th	LESDAIN	Marched to LESDAIN	
		Lieut. S. ATTENBOROUGH posted to Trench Mortars, 33rd Div, with effect from 29.9.18	
25th	-do-	Rev. R.H. RIDSDALE, C.F. (attached) left to join 46th Div.	
25th	do	150 O.R. British Personnel -as authorised in a D.A.C by W.E. No 1556 dy – 7/8/18 – joined from BASE Depot.	
30th	-do-	Lieut. D.K. FLINT joined on posting from 162 Bde R.F.A. with effect from 22nd inst. 2/Lt A.B. JINKS posted from 156 Bde R.F.A. will report from 24th inst.	
		Casualties during month —
Died of Wounds – 3 O.R.
Wounded – 1 O.R.
Died – 1 O.R. (Influenza)	

Lt Col Commdg. 33rd Divl Ammn Column
T.2.xii.1918

Army Form C. 2118.

33 D.A.C.

One Sheet

WAR DIARY
or
INTELLIGENCE SUMMARY.
(Erase heading not required.)

Hour, Date, Place	Summary of Events and Information	Remarks and references to Appendices
	DECEMBER 1918.	
FRIDAY, 6th LESDAINS	Column marched to EQUANCOURT and bivouacked for night.	
SATURDAY 7th EQUANCOURT	Continued march to MEAULTE.	
SUNDAY, 8th MEAULTE	Marched to PONT NOYELLES	
MONDAY, 9th PONT NOYELLES	Marched to LA CHAUSSEE	
TUESDAY, 10th LA CHAUSSEE	Marched to ANDAINVILLE	
THURSDAY, 12th ANDAINVILLE	Marched to NEUVILLE - COPPEQUEULE, HONROY and took up permanent billets.	
SATURDAY, 21st NEUVILLE	Rev. P.S. INGRAM M.C. C.F. joined from BASE for duty with the D.A. Arty, now attached to D.A.C.	
TUESDAY, 31st — DO —	The Division inspected by the Divisional Commander, Maj. Gen. Sir R. PINNEY. K.C.B.	
	DEMOBILIZED during month — MINERS - 18 O.R. BRITAL MEN - 2 O.R.	

J Forbes
Colonel
Comdg. 33 D.A.C. R.F.A.

1st January 1919.

Army Form C. 2118.

33D Am Col

WAR DIARY
or
INTELLIGENCE SUMMARY.
(Erase heading not required.)

Instructions regarding War Diaries and Intelligence Summaries are contained in F.S. Regs., Part II. and the Staff Manual respectively. Title pages will be prepared in manuscript.

JJ 38

Hour, Date, Place	Summary of Events and Information	Remarks and references to Appendices
18.1.19 IN THE FIELD	CAPT. C. MOORE & LIEUT. O.E. CAUSER to Dispersal Station.	(A)
19.1.19	CAPT. N. SMITH to Dispersal Station	(A)
20.1.19	BT. COLONEL L. FORDE. SNS to ENGLAND (DEMOB.)	(A)
30.1.19	LIEUT. H.M. FOULSHAM and 20 O.R.s attached from 33RD. D. T.M. BATTERIES.	(A)
31.1.19	LIEUT. F.C. ROSE. posted to S.A.A. SECTION from 162 BDE. R.F.A.	(A)
31.1.19	2LT. N.T.C. EVANS (No.2 SECTION) Evacuated to ENGLAND, from Hospital.	(A)
31.1.19	31 HORSES & 161 MULES, CLASS "Z" sent to No. 7 VET. HOSPITAL, FORGES LES EAU, for demobilization. 116 Other Ranks demobilised during the month of JANUARY.	(A)

Allen Capt. R.F.A.
(Comdg. 33D Div. Ammn. Column.)

17

Army Form C. 2118.

WAR DIARY
or
INTELLIGENCE SUMMARY.
(Erase heading not required.)

33rd D.A.C. R.F.A.

Hour, Date, Place	Summary of Events and Information	Remarks and references to Appendices
NEUVILLE - COPPEGUEULE.		V51 39
8th February 1919.	Lieut. T.C. Rose R.F.A. proceeded to England for demobilization.	
11th " " 1919.	Lieut. A.M. Jonkhans R.F.A. was posted to 33rd D.A.C. R.F.A.	33rd Div. Arty. R.O. No. 2131.
7th " " 1919.	38 horses were sent away from 33rd A.C. to forges-les-Eaux for sale.	
12th " " 1919.	44 animals were sent away to 33rd D.A.C. for repatriation.	
	111 Remount depot Rouen.	
	During the month of February 1919, 30 other ranks have been demobbed.	

J.A. Moulapha
2nd Lieut
Comdg 33rd D.A.C.

Army Form C. 2118.

WAR DIARY
or
INTELLIGENCE SUMMARY.
(Erase heading not required.)

Instructions regarding War Diaries and Intelligence Summaries are contained in F. S. Regs., Part II. and the Staff Manual respectively. Title pages will be prepared in manuscript.

Wil 40

Hour, Date, Place	Summary of Events and Information	Remarks and references to Appendices
1/3/19 to 31/3/19 NEUVILLET-COPPEGUEULE (SOMME)	312 Animals demobilized during the month. 6 Other Ranks " " " "	AB AB
17.3.19 NEUVILLE-COPPE (SOMME)	40 "Z" Animals received from Regt.l.P.A.H. Abr.	AB

Capt. R.F.A.
Reg. 93rd B.A.C.

Army Form C. 2118.

WAR DIARY
or
INTELLIGENCE SUMMARY.
(Erase heading not required.)

33rd D.A.C. R.F.A.

Hour, Date, Place	Summary of Events and Information	Remarks and references to Appendices
7th April 1919.	5 "Z" animals despatched for Remount Depot Abbeville.	
1st April 1919.	Lieut. A.E. Phipps joined 33rd D.A.C. R.F.A. from H.Q. 33rd Div. Arty.	33rd R.A.R.O. 2146 dated 2/4/19.
7th April 1919.	Lieut. S.R. Woodcock appointed A/Adj of 33rd D.A.C. vice A/Capt. A.B. Jervis.	33rd R.A.R.O. 2147 dated 8/4/19.
9th April 1919.	A/Capt. F.J. Bush proceeded with ad draft to 62nd Division.	33rd D.A. No. S/67 dated 18/3/19.
23rd April 1919.	4 "Z" animals despatched for transfer to 33rd Div. Signals.	
30th April 1919.	19 O.Rs demobilized during the month of April 1919. 33rd D.A.C. R.F.A. billeted in NEUVILLE-COPPEGUEULE.	

J. Allen Major R.F.A.
Commanding Divisional Ammunition Column
33rd DIVISION

Army Form C. 2118.

33RD. D.A.C., R.F.A

WAR DIARY
or
INTELLIGENCE SUMMARY.
(Erase heading not required.)

Instructions regarding War Diaries and Intelligence Summaries are contained in F.S. Regs., Part II. and the Staff Manual respectively. Title pages will be prepared in manuscript.

Hour, Date, Place	Summary of Events and Information	Remarks and references to Appendices
16TH, 17TH & 18TH MAY 1919	Moved from NEUVILLE-COPPEGUEULE, (SOMME) to GAMACHES (SOMME)	
16TH. MAY 1919 GAMACHES	50 other ranks dispersed. Capt. W.R.WOODCOCK (SR) in charge of dispersed draft.	
17TH. MAY 1919 GAMACHES	2/Lt. D.W.FLINT, Lieut H.M.FOULSHAM & 21 other ranks dispersed.	

J.Allen Major R.F.A.
O.g. 33rd. D.A.C. R.F.A.

Army Form C. 2118.

X.A.C. RFA
33rd

WAR DIARY or INTELLIGENCE SUMMARY.

(Erase heading not required.)

Instructions regarding War Diaries and Intelligence Summaries are contained in F.S. Regs., Part II and the Staff Manual respectively. Title pages will be prepared in manuscript.

Remarks and references to Appendices

9/52 43

Hour, Date, Place	Summary of Events and Information	Remarks
Barracks		
10th June 1919	1st Half cadre, 51 men, proceeded to England for demobilization.	
11th June 1919	2nd Half cadre 47 men, proceeded to England for demobilization, leaving equipment guard of 65 men.	

Myrone Cole Capt RFA
Ady 33rd X.A.C.

www.ingramcontent.com/pod-product-compliance
Lightning Source LLC
Chambersburg PA
CBHW081550160426
43191CB00011B/1892